Buckle Down!®
on Virginia History and Social Science
Book 8

Buckle Down
PUBLISHING COMPANY

Acknowledgments

Abigail Adams portrait, from an original painting by Gilbert Stuart, reprinted courtesy of the Library of Congress, Prints and Photographs Division, reproduction number LC-USZ62-10016. Public domain.

"Sacajawea Monument in City Park, Portland, Oregon." Statue by Alice Cooper, 1912. Reprinted courtesy of the Library of Congress, Prints and Photographs Division, reproduction number LC-USZ62-93141.

Photograph of the arm and torch of Bartholdi's Statue of Liberty at the 1876 Philadelphia World's Fair from the Larson Collection, Sanoian Special Collections Library, Henry Madden Library, California State University, Fresno.

"Two officials of the New York City Tenement House Department inspect a cluttered basement living room," photograph circa 1900 reprinted courtesy of the National Archives and Records Administration, control number NWDNS-196-GS-32.

World War I photograph of American engineers returning from the front of the Battle of St. Mihiel by the Bureau of Indian Affairs. Reprinted courtesy of the National Archives and Records Administration, Central Plains Region, control number NRE-75-HAS(PHO)-63. Public domain.

"Norris Dam at Work," photograph reprinted courtesy of the New Deal Network (http://newdeal.feri.org).

"Civil Rights March on Washington D.C. [Entertainment: closeup view of vocalists Joan Baez and Bob Dylan]" photograph by the U.S. Information Agency. Reprinted courtesy of the National Archives and Records Administration, control number NWDNS-306-SSM-4C(53)24. Public domain.

"Suffrage Parade, New York City, May 6, 1912," photograph reprinted courtesy of the Library of Congress, Prints and Photographs Division, reproduction number LC-USZ62-10845.

Edsel billboard "Impressive, yes! Expensive, no!" reprinted courtesy of Publications International, Ltd.

Economic systems table copyright ©1999 by Roberta Eide. Used with permission.

"Republican presidential candidate Senator Phil Gramm faced a media blitz after appearing at a rally at the state capital Wednesday." Photo by David Peterson. Copyright © 1996 by the Des Moines Register and Tribune Company. Reprinted with permission.

History and Social Science Standards of Learning for Virginia Public Schools, copyright © 1995 by the Virginia Board of Education. Used with permission.

ISBN 0-7836-2004-7

Catalog #BD VA8SS 1   4 5 6 7 8 9 10

President and Publisher: Douglas J. Paul, Ph.D.; Editorial Director: John Hansen; Project Editor: James A. Bartlett; Contributing Editors: Rick Zollo, Greta Anderson, Ted Remington; Production Editor: Michael Hankes; Production Director: Jennifer Booth; Art Director: Chris Wolf; Graphic Designer: Kim Life.

Cover image: © 1997 PhotoDisc, Inc.

TABLE OF CONTENTS

Appendix

UNIT I

Above: *The first European explorers arrived in the New World on ships like this one. Their arrival changed both the New World and the old one.*

U.S. History and Geography: First Contact to 1877

The next time you're outdoors, look around you and try to imagine how it must have looked 500 years ago. There were no metal and concrete buildings, no paved streets and highways, no traffic noise, and no bicycles. Instead, the world was filled with trees, meadows, and streams. Animals rustled through forests and birds soared among the trees. There were people here, too.

Only later did European explorers "discover" the New World the American Indians already knew. These Europeans turned loose mighty changes on the life and land of North America. They brought new ideas about the economy, religion, and government. They created a new country, the United States, unlike any country the world had seen before. It's not a perfect country; it never was. Yet its history is one of the great success stories in all the world.

This unit looks back over some of that history.

1

Lesson 1

The First Americans

IT'S IMPORTANT:

■ American Indians had diverse cultures but shared some beliefs.

■ Nations of the North and West included the Inuits and Anasazi.

■ The Iroquois were an important nation of the Northeast.

■ Aztecs and Mayans lived in Central America.

Native Americans had been living in North America for thousands of years when Christopher Columbus traveled to America in 1492. Columbus called them "Indians" because he thought he'd reached India. He also called them "red men" because they painted their faces red.

Scientists believe that Native Americans came from Asia. At one time, the Pacific Ocean did not cover the region between Asia and Alaska. Sometime around 15,000 years ago, people probably crossed the "land bridge" between the two continents and began moving south.

At the time of Columbus, four to six million American Indians lived in North America. They spoke about 250 different languages. Their ways of life and their beliefs also were different. **Inuits** in the cold, icy North, for example, had to live differently than **Pueblos** in the hot, dry Southwest. The way the different groups lived depended greatly on their environment. What lived and grew around them would decide what they ate, made, and traded with others.

Common Beliefs

Most American Indians tribes believed in many different **spirits** who ruled from an unseen world. Some tribes believed that one **Great Spirit** ruled all the other spirits.

All American Indians felt connected to nature. Because the Indians depended on the land for food and shelter, nature was part of their religion. (A Navajo blessing says, "Earth's body has become my body.") They prayed to different spirits for good hunting and good crops. Many tribes believed that the spirits of their dead ancestors lived near them in nature.

In most tribes, men did the hunting. In the many tribes that farmed, women often grew the corn and other crops. Families did not hunt and grow crops only for

> *Mother, Father, you who belong to the Great Beings, you who belong to the Storm Clouds, you will help me. I am ready to put down yellow corn and also blue corn. Therefore you will help me and you will make my work light. Also you will make the field not hard. You will make it soft.*
> —Pueblo planting prayer

Native American Cultures

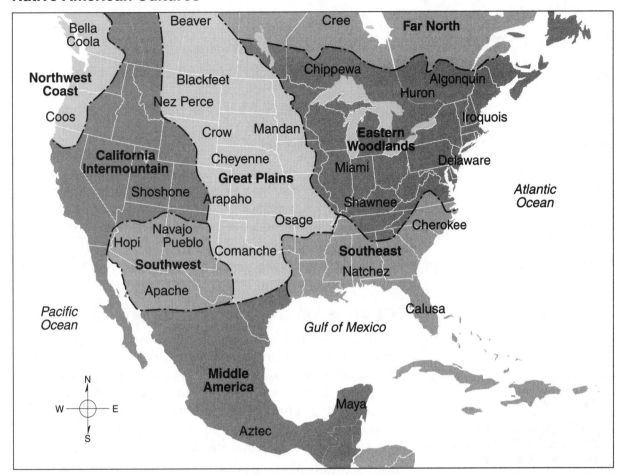

themselves; each family shared its crops with the entire tribe. Whether American Indians lived together in small groups of 25 people or large villages of 2,000 people, most of them shared food and other things.

Chiefs or leaders governed the tribes. Leaders, however, could stay in power only if the people liked what they were doing. In some tribes, the women selected the leaders.

Quick Review 1: Briefly describe common American Indians beliefs about the following:

Spirits:

_____

_____

_____

Food:

_____

_____

_____

Leadership:

_____

_____

_____

Inuit Facts

The Inuits are sometimes called "Eskimos," but never by the Inuits themselves. "Eskimo" is a French mispronunciation of an Algonquin Indian word meaning "eaters of raw meat."

The Inuits were less interested in religion than many other native groups. They didn't like to talk about spirits, fearing that most trouble was caused by them. Many Inuits were eager to convert to Christianity because missionaries told them they would be safe from spirits if they did.

Today, the Inuit population is largely in eastern and central Canada. Their lands are part of the new Canadian territory of Nunavut.

Nations of the West and North

The Inuits live in the far north, from northern Alaska through northern Canada to Greenland. They are probably not related to most other Native American groups. They have more in common with the Asian people of Siberia. Because they live in cold climates, they developed special technology for hunting, fishing, traveling, and living in the cold, such as the kayak and the igloo.

Hunting and fishing also were important to the American Indians of the northwestern United States, including the Kwakiutls, Coos, and Bella Coolas. These tribes almost always built their villages on bodies of water and traveled by boat.

Each tribe was led by a few important families. These families entertained each other at feasts called potlatches. A **potlatch** also could celebrate a wedding or other social event. Sometimes, the celebrations lasted for days. Potlatches are still held in some northwestern American Indian communities today.

The Anasazi lived in the Four Corners region of the United States, where the modern-day states of Utah, Colorado, New Mexico, and Arizona come together. They were a farming people who are sometimes called "cliff dwellers" because of the homes they built on and near the sides of cliffs. The Anasazi are ancestors of the Pueblo Indians; sometimes the cliff homes are called "pueblos."

Sometime around the year 1300, the Anasazi moved south. The reason is unclear. One historian says they left "as if they meant to return in a few minutes." They left their homes and belongings behind, never to return.

Up Close: On the Hunt

The way the Plains Indians used the buffalo is a good example of the way Indians depended on nature to meet their needs. The buffalo was huge, weighing at least 1,000 pounds, but it could run and was frightening when it charged. This big, fast, dangerous animal was the main source of food and clothing for the Plains Indians.

Early each summer and late each fall, the Pawnee, Crow, and other Plains Indians hunted the buffalo. Almost every member of the tribe—men, women, and children—went on the hunt. The tribes traveled hundreds of miles, all on foot. (The Spanish brought the horse to America; it was unknown to the Indians.) The men did the actual hunting; the women carried all the supplies.

The Indians planned the buffalo hunt well. First, scouts found the buffalo herd. Then another group of men drove the herd into a pen they had made, where another group of men killed the buffalo. Sometimes they drove the buffalo over a cliff instead.

Each buffalo provided the tribe with about 450 pounds of fresh meat. The tribe also used every other part of the buffalo:

- **Head**: masks
- **Hide**: clothes, blankets, luggage, shelter material
- **Horns**: spoons, bowls
- **Hooves**: glue, rattles
- **Bones**: needles, tools, toys
- **Intestines**: thread, bow strings
- **Bladder**: balls, toys, containers

Native Americans didn't let any part of the buffalo go to waste. They needed all of it and they respected each animal too much to waste any part of it.

Indians believed the animals they killed didn't really die. The animal still lived in the meat the Indians ate. In that way, the Indian and the animal became one.

At one time, millions of buffalo roamed the Great Plains of North America. When buffalo-skin robes became popular among white Americans, buffalo hunting increased.

Other hunters shot the buffalo for fun and left the bodies to rot in the sun. By the 1880s, there were only about 1,000 left. The buffalo has made a comeback in recent years, however. Today, herds of buffalo live on ranches in the Plains.

Quick Review 2: List some facts about each group below.

Inuits: _____

_____

_____

Anasazi:_____

_____

_____

Nations of the Midwest and East

Mound Builders once lived in what is now the middle of the United States, from Iowa to Georgia. They got their name from the giant mounds of earth they built. The Mound Builders often buried their dead in these mounds and used them to support temples and houses. They were a farming and hunting people who traded with other tribes far away.

Studies of the mounds show that the Mound Builders were active about 1,000 years ago. By the time the first Europeans explored the central United States, most of them were gone. No one is sure why the Mound Builders died out. They left behind only their mounds. The mounds were a mystery to Europeans, who had no idea what they were for.

A variety of tribes also lived in the northeastern and north central United States. They include the **Iroquois**, **Algonquins**, and **Chippewas**. Their homelands were usually thick forests, so they were hunters. They also cleared trees to make space for farm fields. They lived together in dome-shaped houses covered with tree bark. The Iroquois lived in long houses with separate rooms for related families.

The tribes of the Northeast often fought with one another. Sometime around the year 1400, an Onondaga chief, Hiawatha, set up the **Iroquois League of Five Nations**. The Onondaga, Mohawk, Oneida, Cayuga, and Seneca tribes agreed to live in peace and work together. Later, when the American colonies first thought about uniting to solve their differences with Britain, the Iroquois League was an example to them.

Quick Review 3: List some facts about each group.

Mound Builders: _____

_____

_____

_____

Iroquois: _____

_____

_____

_____

Nations of Central America

The **Aztecs** of central Mexico turned an enormous swamp into a giant city. **Tenochtitlan** was home to more than 100,000 people. Aztec priests were both religious leaders and scientists. They studied the night sky, made a calendar based on the movements of the sun, moon, and stars, and even built pyramids.

The **Incas** lived in present-day Peru, Equador, and Bolivia in South America. They were builders and engineers. Their temples and forts were earthquake-proof and their road system stretched for hundreds of miles. Their doctors were far ahead of European doctors at the same time in history. They knew about medicines the Europeans hadn't discovered yet.

The **Mayans** ruled the Yucatan Peninsula of Mexico and what is now Guatemala. They traded with other peoples of Central America. They shipped out cotton, salt, crafts, and furs in exchange for precious stones, feathers, and chocolate. The Mayans built pyramids as temples of worship and gave animal and human sacrifices to their gods. Mayan religious festivals were occasions for games, dancing, and feasting.

The Mayan civilization disappeared sometime around the year 1200. The Aztecs and Incas lasted until Spanish explorers wiped them out in the early 1500s.

What Do You Think?

Directions: Answer the question on the lines provided. Be prepared to discuss your answer in class.

The Navajo blessing found on page 2 in the text also said that "Earth's mind has become my mind" and "Earth's voice has become my voice." Is the Navajo attitude toward the earth similar to or different from the attitude of most Americans today? Give reasons for your answer.

_____

_____

_____

_____

_____

_____

_____

_____

_____

_____

_____

_____

_____

_____

_____

Test Your Knowledge

Directions: Label each statement true or false. If the statement is false, explain why on the line below the statement.

1. Native Americans were deeply religious.

   _____

2. In many tribes, women were hunters.

   _____

3. Indian chiefs had complete power over the people they governed.

   _____

4. The first Europeans found mysterious mounds and did not know who built them.

   _____

5. Many Indians felt cut off from their friends and family members who had died.

   _____

Directions: Look at the map on page 3. Name two tribes found in each of the following regions of North America listed.

6. Northeastern United States:

   _____

   _____

7. Canada:

   _____

   _____

8. Western United States:

_____

_____

9. Southern United States:

_____

_____

Lesson 2

Explorers and Colonists

Trade has been an important human activity since the beginning of time. The countries of Europe had a long history of trading with the Orient (China, Japan, India, and the Indies). By the 1400s, merchants were making money from this trade. They brought silk, spices, perfume, jewels, and gold from the Orient and then sold them all over Europe.

Goods from the Orient were expensive. Traders had to travel 3,000 to 7,000 miles on rough roads over mountains and through dangerous country to reach some parts of the Orient. Because traders could cover only a few miles each day, it could take a year or more to reach China, Japan, or India. Every nation in Europe wanted a quicker and cheaper route to the Orient.

A daring sailor named **Christopher Columbus** thought he knew a quicker route. Columbus thought he could reach the Orient in just a few weeks by sailing west. He believed Japan was about 3,000 miles across the ocean from Spain. It took him six years to talk **King Ferdinand** and **Queen Isabella** of Spain into giving him about $14,000 to make the trip. On August 3, 1492, Columbus set sail with 88 men in three tiny ships, the *Niña, Pinta,* and *Santa Maria.*

Columbus didn't know that Japan was almost 12,000 miles away from Spain, not 3,000. Nor did he know that two unknown continents—North America and South America— blocked the way. On October 12, 1492, Columbus landed on an island in the Caribbean Sea off the coast of the unknown continents. He thought he was in India.

Although Columbus never stopped believing he had found a faster way to the Orient, other explorers soon realized that Columbus had discovered a new world. Explorers from France, Spain, England, and the Netherlands looked for a way around the New World in hopes of finding a new route to Asia. Others explored the New World. Some hoped to find gold or to turn the native peoples of the New World into Christians. As one adventurer from Spain said, "We came here to serve God and the king and also to get rich."

IT'S IMPORTANT:

- Europeans wanted a quicker and cheaper trade route to the Orient.

- Columbus discovered America while he was seeking this new route; other explorers followed him.

- European countries set up colonies in America for a variety of reasons.

- American colonies developed differently based on where they were located.

Quick Review 1: Why did Europeans want to find a new route to Asia?

_____

_____

_____

AGE OF EXPLORATION TIMELINE

1492	Christopher Columbus discovers America
1497	John Cabot discovers Newfoundland in east Canada
1513	Juan Ponce de León explores Florida
1513	Vasco Nuñez de Balboa discovers the Pacific Ocean
1519-1522	Ferdinand Magellan sails around the world
1534	Jacques Cartier discovers the St. Lawrence River in Canada
1540-1547	Francisco Coronado explores the southwestern United States
1541	Hernando de Soto crosses the Mississippi River
1609-1610	Henry Hudson discovers the river and bay that are named for him
1673	Jacques Marquette and Louis Joliet discover upper Mississippi River

Colonies in the New World

In 1584, Englishman Richard Hakluyt saw the future. He wrote to Queen Elizabeth I of England, saying "Her Majesty will have good harbors" in America. Hakluyt believed England could get rich by trading "cheap English goods for things of great value that are not thought to be worth much by the natives of America." Those "things of great value" included timber for shipbuilding and furs for clothing.

However they made it, money meant power to the Europeans. Europe would think most highly of the nation with the most colonies and the most money. The Spanish found silver and gold in Mexico and South America. Other countries hoped they would find silver and gold, too. As it turned out, they found different ways to prosper. The French went into the fur trade. English companies founded profitable tobacco farms in Virginia and the Carolinas. The Middle Atlantic colonies (New York, New Jersey, and Pennsylvania) grew corn, wheat, and other crops. Farming was more difficult in New England, where farms were smaller. There, timber and fish were important to the economy.

Religion was another reason for coming to America. Spain set up **missions** to convert native peoples to Christianity. France also sent missionaries to convert the American Indians. In 1620, **pilgrims** from England set up the colony of **Plymouth** so they could worship as they pleased. Maryland was founded for Catholics; Pennsylvania was set up by Quakers.

And so, faraway countries set up colonies in the New World for reasons ranging from gold to God. Except for the Spanish, they didn't find gold. European colonies in America became profitable largely through trade. Citizens of the colonies were mostly farmers, producing the crops that made trade possible.

Quick Review 2: Name the reasons European nations set up colonies in America.

_____

_____

_____

_____

Colonies in the South

In the Jamestown, Virginia, colony, the winter of 1609-1610 was "the starving time." Colonists ate "dogs, cats, snakes, toadstools, horsehides and what not" because they had no other food. Ninety people died. That brought the total dead to 840 since the colony began in 1607. By the spring of 1610, only 60 people were left.

The company running the Virginia colony hoped to make a profit from the crops it sold. The people living in the Virginia colony had different reasons for traveling to the New World. Many hoped to make a new start away from the crowded, tiny farms of England. A few came in the hope of practicing the religion of their choice, but this was less of a concern for Virginia colonists than it was for those who settled elsewhere. Some were even criminals, who had been given the choice of prison in England or transportation across the Atlantic.

After the starving time, the coming of more colonists and supplies from England saved Virginia. In 1613, colonists began growing tobacco. The crop became wildly popular in England and ensured that Virginia would be prosperous.

Tobacco also shaped the way colonies in the South developed. Tobacco was most often grown in large fields, so colonists stopped clustering together in villages. Instead, they lived on farms far away from one another. Being far away from people and services meant that each big farm had to become its own village. The biggest farms were called **plantations**. Plantations produced tobacco as well as other crops, such as rice, cotton, and indigo. These **cash crops** were sold in large amounts on the European market.

It took many workers to produce the plantation crops, but plantations also had their own blacksmiths, carpenters, brick makers, and sawmills. Finding enough people to do the plantation jobs was difficult. Plantation owners thought slaves were the answer. The first slaves—20 Africans—were brought to Virginia in 1619. By 1750, nearly half of the people in Virginia were African Americans. The plantation way of life depended on slave labor. The South depended on the plantation way of life.

Colonies in the North

Like the colonists in Virginia, the colonists in Massachusetts were farmers. (Unlike the Virginia colonists, these farmers grew food mostly for their own use, instead of selling it for cash.) Massachusetts **Puritans**, however, lived close together

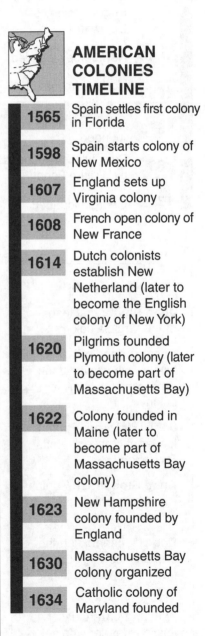

AMERICAN COLONIES TIMELINE

1565	Spain settles first colony in Florida
1598	Spain starts colony of New Mexico
1607	England sets up Virginia colony
1608	French open colony of New France
1614	Dutch colonists establish New Netherland (later to become the English colony of New York)
1620	Pilgrims founded Plymouth colony (later to become part of Massachusetts Bay)
1622	Colony founded in Maine (later to become part of Massachusetts Bay colony)
1623	New Hampshire colony founded by England
1630	Massachusetts Bay colony organized
1634	Catholic colony of Maryland founded

AMERICAN COLONIES TIMELINE

1636	Hartford colony founded (later to become Connecticut); Rhode Island founded by former Puritans
1638	Swedish colonists settle New Sweden (later to become the English colony of Delaware)
1660	New Jersey founded
1663	North Carolina founded
1670	South Carolina founded
1682	Pennsylvania founded by William Penn
1732	Georgia founded

Important People

John Smith: first leader of the Virginia colony

Pocahontas: Indian woman who saved John Smith and the Virginia colony

John Winthrop: Puritan leader of Massachusetts Bay colony

Anne Bradstreet: Puritan who was the first American poet

Roger Williams: left the Puritans for religious freedom in Rhode Island colony

William Penn: Quaker religious leader who set up the Pennsylvania colony

in towns and farmed on land outside the town. Puritans believed it was important to live close together and close to church. That's why they built a **meeting house** in the center of each town.

At the meeting house, Puritans settled community problems and worshipped God. Puritans were strict about their religious beliefs. "Obey the Scriptures in all things," one Puritan advised. Anyone who did not go to church on Sunday faced punishment. Anyone who sang, ran, or jumped on Sunday—the Lord's day—was fined 40 shillings. This was the amount of money most men made in a month. Puritans also believed people should work hard. It was a crime to be lazy.

By working hard and helping each other, Massachusetts colonists succeeded. By 1760, the colony had 222,600 farmers, merchants, fishermen, teachers, and other people. Many of them were not Puritans. The Puritan belief in hard work and close communities, though, influenced the way colonists lived throughout the North.

> *No person shall spend his time unprofitably under pain of punishment.*
> —a law in Puritan New England

Colonies in the Middle

The Middle Atlantic colonies—New York, Pennsylvania, and New Jersey—had a great deal of diversity. Their colonists came from many different European countries. Their farms produced a large variety of crops; the big cities, New York and Philadelphia, were important shipping points for goods. Although slavery was legal, it was not as widespread as in the South.

Quick Review 3: How were colonies in the North different from colonies in the South?

_____

_____

_____

_____

In what ways were they alike?

_____

_____

_____

_____

What Do You Think?

Directions: Read the passage, then use it to answer the question. Be prepared to discuss your answer in class.

The Puritans of Plymouth and the Massachusetts Bay colony came to America to worship as they pleased. A few colonists, led by Roger Williams, wanted to worship as they pleased, but their beliefs were not the same as those of the Puritans. In 1636, the Puritans forced Williams to leave Massachusetts Bay. He and his followers founded the colony of Rhode Island, where each citizen could worship as he or she pleased.

Which group—the Puritans or the colonists of Rhode Island—had the biggest influence on how we think about religion today? Give reasons for your answer.

_____

_____

_____

_____

_____

Test Your Knowledge

Directions: Respond to your choice of one of the two statements. Be as complete as possible. You may use an additional sheet of paper if necessary.

1. You are a sailor traveling with Christopher Columbus. Write a letter to your father back home in Spain. Explain how Columbus was able to make the voyage and what he found when he landed.

2. You are a settler in the Massachusetts Bay colony. Write a letter to your sister back home in England. Explain why you came to Massachusetts Bay and what your life is like in the New World.

_____

_____

_____

_____

_____

_____

_____

_____

_____

_____

_____

_____

_____

_____

Lesson 3

The American Revolution

For almost 200 years, Great Britain, France, and Spain controlled most of the land in North America. Britain (also called England) and France were old enemies. They fought many wars against one another, all around the world.

After the French and Indian War ended in 1763, France gave up most of its lands in North America. Britain gained a big piece of eastern North America to go along with its colonies. Spain received the territory of Louisiana from France. As part of the deal, Spain gave Florida to Britain. France kept some small islands.

Quick Review 1: Which two countries controlled most of the land in North America after 1763?

The Colonies Pay the Price

People from many countries lived in the 13 colonies, but the governments of all the colonies were British. Most of the colonists thought of themselves as British citizens and were loyal to **King George III** of England. Many had fought in the British army against the French.

The French and Indian War cost the British government a lot of money. They decided that the colonists should help pay for the war. After all, the colonists would benefit the most, now that the French were gone.

England began enforcing strict laws on colonial trade to make sure every penny of tax money was collected. They also made it illegal for settlers to move beyond the Appalachian Mountains. This was done to keep colonists from fighting with Native American tribes. This fighting usually required British soldiers to stop it. The British government would have to pay for them.

Great Britain had always let the colonial governments make most of their own decisions, including whether to tax their citizens, but not this time. Many colonists were angered by the new laws. They believed the new laws violated their rights as Englishmen. Some colonists protested them. Others just ignored them.

IT'S IMPORTANT:

■ After the French and Indian War, Great Britain began putting new taxes on its American colonies.

■ Colonists were angered by the taxes, especially in Boston.

■ Colonists organized groups of Minutemen to defend themselves from Britain.

■ The first battles of the Revolution were fought before the Declaration of Independence was signed.

■ The Declaration of Independence, written by Thomas Jefferson, was signed on July 4, 1776.

■ Six years of war ended with the British surrender at Yorktown and the Treaty of Paris.

Division of Land, 1763

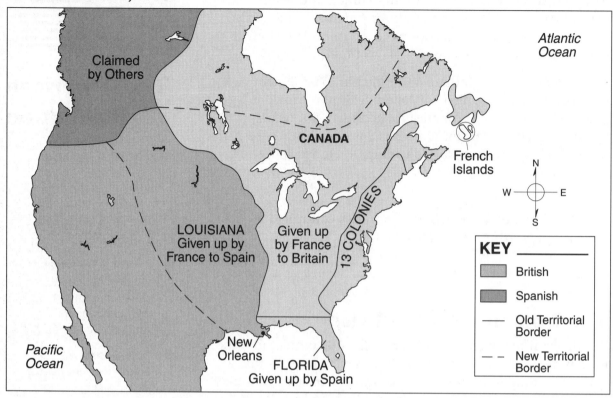

Quick Review 2: How did the British government upset the people of the colonies after the French and Indian War?

_____

_____

_____

Taxation without Representation

Starting in 1764, the British government began putting more taxes on the colonists. The **Sugar Act** (1764), the **Stamp Act** (1765), and the **Townshend Acts** (1767) required colonists to pay taxes on things they used every day, like sugar, newspapers, and tea.

A group called the **Sons of Liberty** organized protests against the taxes. People boycotted taxed goods, which means they refused to buy them. The boycotts worked. In 1770, the last of the taxes were repealed (ended), except for a small tax on tea.

Nobody likes to pay taxes. What made the colonists most angry about these taxes, though, was that they had no representatives in the British Parliament to speak for them. If they had had the right to argue and vote against the taxes, they might have been more willing to accept them. "Taxation without representation," they said, "is tyranny." **Tyranny** means ruling unfairly by not following the law.

Boston Boils Over

Boston, Massachusetts, was the biggest city in the colonies. It also was home to a large number of British soldiers. In March of 1770, a crowd of citizens got into a shouting match with a group of soldiers. The soldiers fired their guns, and five townspeople were killed. This event became known as the **Boston Massacre**.

In 1773, Parliament, led by Prime Minister **Lord Frederick North**, passed a new Tea Act, which hurt colonial companies in the tea business. Tea was the most popular drink in the colonies, but many people stopped drinking it.

To protest the act, people in New York and Philadelphia forced British tea ships to turn around and go home. In Boston, citizens kept tea ships from unloading. Then, on December 16, 1773, citizens disguised as American Indians boarded a tea ship and quietly dumped its cargo of tea into Boston Harbor. The event became known as the **Boston Tea Party**.

The First Continental Congress

The Boston Tea Party caused Parliament to punish Boston with new laws. The rights of citizens were greatly restricted. The laws punishing Boston soon became known as the **Intolerable Acts**.

In September of 1774, the **First Continental Congress** was held in Philadelphia. Representatives from 12 of the 13 colonies met to strongly protest the Intolerable Acts. (Only Georgia was absent.) The colonies agreed not to trade with England or use British goods until the acts were repealed. They agreed to meet again in the spring of 1775 if their complaints weren't settled by then.

The colonists just wanted their rights as English citizens. They wanted to be governed and taxed by their colonial governments, but they were willing to let the king have the last word on any taxes. The First Continental Congress did not plan for independence in the fall of 1774.

AMERICAN REVOLUTION TIMELINE

1763	French and Indian War ends
1765	Stamp Act puts tax on paper goods; Sons of Liberty organize protests
1767	Townshend Acts put tax on lead, paper, glass, paint, and tea
1770	March: British soldiers kill citizens in Boston Massacre
1773	May: Tea Act passed
1773	December: Colonists destroy tea at Boston Tea Party
1774	Spring: Intolerable Acts passed to punish Boston
1774	September: First Continental Congress meets
1775	April: Battle of Lexington and Concord
1775	May: Second Continental Congress meets; George Washington put in command of Continental Army
1775	June: Battle of Bunker Hill in Boston
1776	July: Declaration of Independence is approved
1777-1778	Winter: Continental Army suffers at Valley Forge
1781	British surrender after being trapped at Yorktown
1783	Treaty of Paris ends the Revolutionary War

Quick Review 3: What did the First Continental Congress do?

_____

_____

Patrick Henry

On March 23, 1775, **Patrick Henry** made a speech at a political convention in Virginia. Tensions were high. The battle of Lexington and Concord was less than a month away. Henry believed the British would never give the colonies their rights and that there was no way to avoid a war.

He asked his fellow Virginians: "Is life so dear, or peace so sweet, as to be purchased at the price of chains and slavery?" In his opinion, it was not. "I know not what course others may take, but as for me, give me liberty or give me death!"

Many Americans today share Henry's belief that they'd rather die than give up their liberty.

"If They Mean to Have a War, Let It Begin Here!"

Many Massachusetts colonists didn't believe that Parliament would hear their protests. They began organizing into groups called **Minutemen**. They took their name because they said they would be ready to fight within a minute's notice.

The British knew exactly what was happening. General **Thomas Gage**, commander of British troops in America, had been named governor of Massachusetts. Gage was not going to let a rebellion start while he was in charge. He wanted the rebel leaders, including **Samuel Adams** and **John Hancock**, arrested. He planned to send British soldiers to Lexington, near Boston, to round them up.

On the night of April 18, 1775, some colonists found out what Gage was planning. Three of them, **Paul Revere**, **William Dawes**, and **Samuel Prescott**, rode through the countryside to warn the Minutemen that the British were coming. The next morning, a group of Minutemen marched into place in Lexington. Their captain said, "Stand your ground. Don't fire unless fired upon; but if they mean to have a war, let it begin here!" Soon the British soldiers, wearing their red uniforms, marched into Lexington. The officer leading them ordered the Minutemen to go home, but they refused to move.

No historian is sure which side fired first, but someone did. Eighteen Minutemen were killed or wounded. The British marched a few miles to **Concord**, where they fought more Minutemen. As the British marched back to Boston, angry colonists fired on them all along the way. By the end of the day, 273 British soldiers, called Redcoats for the color of their uniforms, had been killed or wounded, compared to 93 Americans.

Fighting for Rights as Englishmen

The **Second Continental Congress** met in May of 1775. Even though blood had been spilled, the American colonists still did not speak openly about becoming independent. They insisted they were still loyal to King George. They sent a message to him, asking for his help to settle the differences between the colonies and Parliament.

At the same time, however, the Congress formed the Continental Army. It would be led by a Virginia soldier named **George Washington**. The Congress asked the other colonies to send men and money to pay for the war effort.

Fighting went on in many places during 1775. In Boston, the colonists won the **Battle of Bunker Hill**. There was fighting in New York, the Carolinas, and Virginia, too. But the colonists still hoped they could settle their differences with the British.

Independence

King George III did not help the colonists. He insisted that they obey Parliament. He closed the colonies to all trade and sent even more soldiers. The Continental Congress looked for help from other countries. They organized a navy to attack British ships. In June of 1776, a Virginia representative named **Richard Henry Lee** proposed that the "United Colonies" should become independent because there was no way they could ever patch up their differences with Great Britain.

The Congress formed a committee to write a **Declaration of Independence**. Most of it was written by **Thomas Jefferson**, a 33-year-old Virginia representative. The Declaration explained what Americans believed and why they had the right to be free and independent. On July 2, 1776, the Congress voted in favor of the Declaration. It was signed on July 4. (You'll read more about the Declaration of Independence in Lesson 16.)

Whigs and Tories

As the colonies prepared for revolution, not everyone was willing to fight against Britain. As many as 20 percent of the colonists wanted to remain loyal. These loyalists, also known as **Tories**, came from cities and farm areas, north and south, rich and poor. The strongest loyalist areas were in New York, Georgia, and South Carolina. As many as 60,000 loyalists served in the British army, 15,000 of them around New York City alone. (The Iroquois Indians of New York supported the British as well.)

Those who wanted independence were sometimes known as **Whigs**. Boston was the center of Whig strength, where hatred of the British had led to the Boston Tea Party and the battle of Lexington and Concord. At the same time, however, Massachusetts was home to a large number of loyalists. Virginia was also home to many Whigs, such as Washington, Jefferson, and James Madison. Most Virginians lost interest in being loyal in 1775, when the royal governor urged slaves to leave their masters and fight for the king.

Many loyalists had business, religious, or governmental ties to Britain. Others simply argued that Britain was the strongest country in the world. They asked why Americans should give up their British citizenship to become citizens of a new country whose future was uncertain.

For Tories and Whigs whose families and communities were divided, the Revolutionary War was a civil war. Between 80,000 and 100,000 loyalists left the colonies. Many went to Canada, where they could remain subjects of the British Empire.

The United States (1783)

Above: *North America after the Revolutionary War, 1783*

Women of the Revolution

In the spring of 1776, the 13 colonies were heading toward a revolution. One of the leaders was John Adams of Massachusetts. One day, Adams opened a letter from his wife, Abigail.

In the letter, Abigail told John that she looked forward to hearing that independence had been declared. She also had a message for the leaders of the new country as they got ready to make laws to govern it. "Remember the ladies and be more generous and favorable to them," Abigail Adams wrote. "Do not put such unlimited power into the hands of the husbands."

The men who led the Revolution did not take Abigail Adams's advice. Women were still not allowed to vote, own property, or attend school in the new United States. However, many American women supported the Revolution anyway. They stuck to the boycotts of British goods in the years before the war. After the war began, farm women took care of their families and farms while their husbands were away. In towns and cities, other women managed their husbands' businesses while they fought the British. At the same time, women managed chores at home and held their families together. They often gave shelter, food, and supplies to Washington's troops.

Abigail Adams

Other women helped the war effort directly. A group called the Daughters of Liberty sewed clothes for the troops; the Ladies Association raised money. Benjamin Franklin's daughter, Sarah Franklin Bache, joined other women of Philadelphia to raise $300,000 to assist soldiers. Sixteen-year-old Sybil Ludington rode twice as far as Paul Revere had to warn Minutemen and citizens that the British were coming to Danbury, Connecticut. Margaret Corbin followed her husband into the Continental Army to do cooking, washing, and nursing. When Corbin's husband was killed, she took over the firing of his cannon. Deborah Sampson disguised herself as a man and enlisted. Lydia Darragh took the dangerous job of spying for the Continental Army.

After the war, women's wartime experiences led to the opening of private schools for young girls. Some women agreed with Abigail Adams and began working for equal rights. Obtaining those rights would be a long, slow process.

A New Nation

It wasn't enough for the Americans to say they were independent. They had to win their independence in war.

The British had a bigger, more powerful, better-trained army than the Americans. But soldiers in the American army were fighting for freedom and showed great dedication to their cause. The winter at **Valley Forge** is an example. Washington took his army to Valley Forge, Pennsylvania, to spend the winter of 1777-1778. The soldiers suffered through the cold with little food, no warm clothing, and poor shelter. Although some soldiers quit, enough of them stayed so that the war could go on when spring came.

After Valley Forge, the war was mostly over in the northern colonies. During the next three years, fighting would take place in the southern colonies, ending with the defeat of the British at **Yorktown**, Virginia. On October 17, 1781, Washington's army trapped a British force led by **Lord Charles Cornwallis**.

Even before Yorktown, the English people were getting tired of the faraway war. After Yorktown, Parliament voted to begin peace talks. In the **Treaty of Paris**, signed in 1783, Britain recognized the independence of the United States. All the land from the Atlantic Ocean to the Mississippi River and from Canada to Florida became American territory.

Independence had been won. Now the leaders of the new country had a big job ahead. They would have to create a government that could live up to the ideas of the Declaration of Independence.

The leaders of the new country also had a big problem. Even though they had won the Revolutionary War, the United States of America was not strong or powerful, especially when compared to England, France, and Spain. All three countries would be watching. If the United States were to fall apart, any one of the three would be glad to pick up the pieces.

Quick Review 4: Why was the United States still in danger even after winning the Revolutionary War?

_____

_____

_____

What Do You Think?

Directions: Answer the questions on the lines provided. Be prepared to discuss your answers in class.

1. Were the colonists right to protest British taxes or should they have done what their government told them to do? Give reasons for your answer.

_____

_____

_____

2. Even after the battle of Lexington and Concord, the colonists hoped to solve their disagreements with Parliament. Could they have done it? Give reasons for your answer.

_____

_____

_____

Test Your Knowledge

Directions: Answer the questions on the lines provided.

1. Why did the British begin putting taxes on the colonists after 1763?

_____

_____

_____

2. How did the colonists respond to the taxes placed on them by the British?

_____

_____

_____

3. At the time of the First Continental Congress, what did the colonists want?

_____

_____

_____

_____

4. What finally made the colonists decide to declare their independence?

_____

_____

_____

_____

5. Give one of the two reasons why the British surrendered at Yorktown and ended the Revolutionary War.

_____

_____

_____

_____

The first four presidents of the United States were **George Washington**, **John Adams**, **Thomas Jefferson**, and **James Madison**. The first three had been important leaders of the Revolution; Madison had been the "Father of the Constitution." Their job was to guide the new country through its growing pains. They faced trouble at home and with other countries. Often, they had to make up the rules as they went along.

Money

The United States had struggled to pay its bills ever since it was born. When the Constitution went into effect, the country owed millions to foreign countries and its own citizens. The first Secretary of the Treasury, **Alexander Hamilton**, had a plan for solving these problems. The government would pay the bills over a period of time and create some new taxes to raise more money. The United States also would run its own bank to handle the government's money.

The bank and the taxes made some Americans angry. Some citizens, including **Thomas Jefferson**, feared that the bank would be too powerful. It would favor the rich and harm the poor. Smaller, local banks should handle the country's money. Jefferson also believed the Constitution did not allow Congress to set up such a bank. Hamilton disagreed with Jefferson. In 1791, the **Bank of the United States** went into business.

Jefferson and Hamilton had disagreed before. Hamilton favored the strong government set up by the Constitution; Jefferson believed it was too strong. The bank debate opened the old disagreements and led to the forming of two **political parties**. Those Americans who agreed with Hamilton called themselves **Federalists**. Those who agreed with Jefferson called themselves **Democratic-Republicans**.

In 1794, farmers in Pennsylvania refused to pay the tax on whiskey, a drink made from corn. They also promised to hurt the tax collectors. President **George Washington** sent an army to force the farmers to pay. The quick end to the **Whiskey Rebellion** showed that the new, young government was strong enough to make its citizens obey the law.

Lesson 4

The Early Republic

IT'S IMPORTANT:

- A disagreement between Alexander Hamilton and Thomas Jefferson over how to solve the nation's money troubles led to the first political parties.

- The United States fought a small war with France starting in 1798 and a bigger one with Great Britain starting in 1812.

- The Alien and Sedition Acts limited free speech.

- The Louisiana Purchase increased the size of the United States.

Quick Review 1: How did the Bank of the United States help create political parties in the United States?

_____

_____

Enemies

The new United States was a weak country in a world full of strong ones. Britain, France, and Spain were all much more powerful. The new government tried to make sure none of the three would harm the country. In 1793, when France fought against Britain and Spain, Washington announced that the United States would remain **neutral** and not get involved. The United States also made **treaties** (agreements) with the Europeans, although the Europeans sometimes broke them.

At first, the relationship with France was the worst. The U.S. Navy fought a small war with France from 1798 to 1800, while John Adams was president. There would be a bigger war while President Madison was in office. In 1812, disagreements between the United States and Britain turned to war for the second time in less than 40 years. The **War of 1812** was fought mostly at sea along the Atlantic Coast and on the Great Lakes. The British burned the White House and the Capitol in Washington, D.C. On the frontier, the war was between white settlers and American Indians, who sometimes supported the British. Neither Britain nor America was a clear winner, but the United States settled many of its differences with Britain in the peace treaty.

Quick Review 2: How was the War of 1812 really two wars?

_____

_____

_____

PRESIDENTS

1789	George Washington elected
1792	Washington re-elected
1796	Washington retires; John Adams elected
1800	Thomas Jefferson defeats Adams
1804	Jefferson re-elected
1808	Jefferson retires; James Madison elected
1816	Madison retires; James Monroe elected

Speaking Freely

In 1798, American problems with France were at their worst. Many Americans feared that their country would not survive. John Adams, a member of the Federalist party, was president. Federalists also controlled the Congress. Hoping to make the country safer against foreign threats, the Federalists passed the **Alien and Sedition** (*sed-ISH-un*) **Acts**.

An **alien** is a person who lives in a country but is not a citizen of that country. The Alien and Sedition Acts raised the length of time needed for an alien to become a citizen from five to 14 years. The acts also gave the president the power to order aliens to leave the country if he thought they were dangerous. This part of the law angered the Democratic-Republican party because many immigrants were members of the party.

A person who tries to make others rebel against lawful authority is guilty of **sedition**. The Alien and Sedition Acts made it a crime to criticize the government or government officials. This seemed to go against the First Amendment. Even so, several newspaper editors were thrown in jail for printing stories that disagreed with the government or its actions.

Many Americans wondered if there was anything they could do if Congress passed a bad law. Some, including James Madison and Thomas Jefferson, believed that states could decide whether to obey federal laws. This idea, known as **states' rights**, would cause conflict in the coming years whenever states disagreed with actions of the federal government. By 1861, it would lead to the Civil War.

The Sedition Act quietly disappeared after Jefferson, a Democratic-Republican, became president in 1801. In 1803, the United States Supreme Court ruled that it had the right to throw out laws that went against the Constitution. Federal courts have used the power of **judicial review** ever since.

The Louisiana Purchase

In 1803, President Jefferson made the greatest real estate deal in history. The United States bought the territory of Louisiana from France. For $15 million, all the land between the Mississippi River and the Rocky Mountains became American territory. The **Louisiana Purchase** made the United States twice as large as before.

Jefferson wanted to find out what kind of place the Louisiana Territory was. He sent a group of explorers, led by **Meriwether Lewis** and **William Clark**, to travel up the Mississippi and Missouri rivers, across the Rockies, and all the way to the Pacific Ocean. With the help of a Shoshone woman named **Sacagawea**, they discovered new plants, animals, and places on their journey. It took the explorers more than two years (1804-1806) to get to the ocean and back home again. The new American territory was rich and beautiful, and people became eager to settle there.

FAST FACT

The Alien Act stayed in effect long after the Sedition Act. The government used it in 1942, when American officials ordered Japanese Americans living on the West Coast to leave their homes and move into internment camps. The government feared that Japanese Americans might help the Japanese against the United States in World War II.

The Louisiana Purchase (1803)

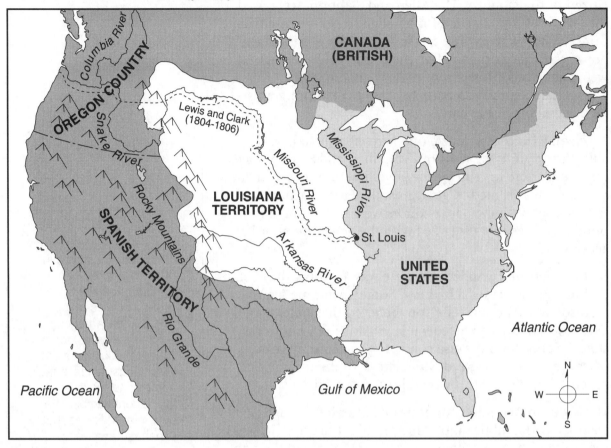

Above: *The Louisiana Purchase and the route of Lewis and Clark*

After the Purchase, the United States grew rapidly. The War of 1812 moved the Indians out of the way of settlement. More new states were added. Great Britain and Spain agreed on treaties that gave the United States pieces of land that make up the map we are familiar with today.

Quick Review 3: Why was the Louisiana Purchase important?

_____

_____

_____

What Do You Think?

Directions: Answer the questions on the lines provided. Be prepared to discuss your answers in class.

1. Why did President Washington think it was a good idea for the United States to stay neutral in the wars involving European countries?

_____

_____

_____

_____

_____

2. How does judicial review complete the system of checks and balances in the Constitution?

_____

_____

_____

_____

_____

Test Your Knowledge

Directions: Complete the timeline with the event that matches each date shown. If there is more than one date shown on the timeline, there is more than one event for that year. To help you, the events are listed below.

EARLY REPUBLIC

| 1791 |
| 1793 |
| 1794 |
| 1798 |
| 1798 |
| 1800 |
| 1803 |
| 1812 |

Jefferson elected president

War at sea against France begins

Alien and Sedition Acts are passed

Bank of the United States is founded

Jefferson makes the Louisiana Purchase

Whiskey Rebellion happens in Pennsylvania

United States and Britain go to war for the second time

Washington says the United States should stay neutral in European wars

Manifest Destiny

In 1800, the United States only extended west from the Atlantic Ocean to the Mississippi River. By 1860, it spread all the way to the Pacific Ocean. The number of people living in the United States jumped from five million in 1800 to 31 million in 1860.

These years were a confident time in American history. Many Americans believed that God had given them the entire North American continent for their great experiment in democracy and freedom. They called the idea **Manifest Destiny**. Manifest Destiny gave Americans the right to settle "from sea to shining sea."

Just because many Americans *thought* they had the right to settle the West didn't mean everyone else agreed with them. Westward expansion led to problems with Great Britain, Mexico, and other countries that believed the land was theirs. It also led to trouble with American Indians who had lived on the land for centuries. Americans themselves quarreled with one another. Some wanted slavery in the West while others did not.

How the Country Grew

There were two ways to travel west in early America: by water or overland. A network of canals linked lakes and rivers in the northeastern United States. For those heading farther west, rivers such as the Ohio, Mississippi, and Missouri were important waterways. Most major American cities grew on water routes, which were the least expensive way to transport people, goods, and services from place to place. For overland travel, several trails had been blazed even before the Revolutionary War. The Wilderness Trail led into Kentucky through the Cumberland Gap; later, the National Road took settlers into Ohio. Going overland was harder than going by water, but it was the best way to reach some places that water routes did not go.

Many factors led people west. It cost very little to buy land in the West. A family who could never hope to own a farm in the area along the Atlantic Ocean might be able to afford a large piece of land in Indiana or Illinois. Some Southern farmers discovered that areas to the west of them were good cotton-growing areas; therefore, they could own larger farms and make more money. Oregon was attractive to settlers because of its good climate and fertile soil.

A few Americans moved simply to be moving. Daniel Boone, an early pioneer of Tennessee and Kentucky, saw too many signs of settlement and announced he was heading for Missouri. Davy Crockett left Tennessee for Texas.

IT'S IMPORTANT:

■ Americans believed it was their "manifest destiny" to spread across the continent.

■ Westward expansion caused problems with other nations and American Indians.

■ The expansion of slavery into new territories led to fighting among Americans.

Quick Review 1: What reasons did Americans have for moving west?

_____

_____

"Remember the Alamo!"

On February 24, 1836, W. Barret Travis wrote from the Alamo: "I am [surrounded] by a thousand or more of the Mexicans . . . . I call on you in the name of Liberty, or patriotism and everything dear to the American character, to come to our aid. . . . If this call is [not heard]. . . . I die like a soldier who never forgets . . . his own honor and that of his country—VICTORY OR DEATH."

Death, not victory, came to Commander Travis and 186 other men defending the Alamo mission near San Antonio, Texas. On March 6, Mexican soldiers finally broke into the Alamo and killed all of those defending it, including the frontier hero Davy Crockett.

The defenders of the Alamo fought for independence from Mexico. Beginning in 1821, Mexico had invited Americans to settle in its Texas territory and become Mexican citizens. By 1835, there were 35,000 Americans in Texas. Most of the Americans were slaveowners. When the Mexican government outlawed slavery, the American settlers rebelled.

The defeat at the Alamo inspired Texans to keep fighting. Later in 1836, they won their independence from Mexico with the battle cry "Remember the Alamo!" The Texans asked the United States to admit them as a new state. Congress did not want to add another slave state in 1836, so for nine years, Texas was an independent country.

Oregon and Mexico

The United States and Great Britain both claimed to own the **Oregon Country**. Stories were told of its good land and beautiful weather, and American settlers were streaming into it.

In 1844, Texas and Oregon were the big issues of the presidential election. Former Tennessee governor **James K. Polk** said that if the voters chose him, he would add both areas to the United States. He was willing to fight Great Britain for Oregon if necessary. Polk won the election. Texas became a state in 1845. The United States and Great Britain peacefully settled their differences over Oregon in 1846.

The Monroe Doctrine

In 1823, President James Monroe announced the Monroe Doctrine. It said that the United States would stay out of Europe's business, so European countries should stay out of North and South America.

Canada was still British territory, however. Britain gave some parts of its territory to the United States through treaties but held on to most of it. As late as 1895, some American leaders hoped for a war with Britain that might allow the United States to take Canada.

The United States and Mexico could not settle their differences peacefully. In 1846, a question of where the border should be between the two countries started the **Mexican War**. The United States army captured Mexican cities and easily won the war. In the 1848 treaty that ended the war, the United States received much of Mexico's northern territory in exchange for about $18 million. Parts of seven states, including California, came from what was known as the **Mexican Cession**. California became very attractive to Americans, especially after gold was discovered in 1848.

By adding the Oregon Country and the Mexican Cession, the United States now reached from the Atlantic to the Pacific. Manifest Destiny had become real, yet problems lay ahead.

Quick Review 2: Which area did the United States take by war?

_____

_____

Which area did it receive peacefully?

_____

_____

Trail of Tears

White Americans saw land as something to own, settle, farm, and build upon. American Indians saw land as a part of nature shared by everyone—something to respect. The different ways in which white Americans and Indians looked at the land led to conflict. Frontier settlers thought that Manifest Destiny gave them the right to take over American Indian homelands.

Indians and settlers made war on each other from the earliest days of settlement. As the United States expanded, its army was called upon to force Indians from land that settlers wanted. Finally, in 1830, president **Andrew Jackson** urged Congress to pass the **Indian Removal Act**. Indians who lived east of the Mississippi River would be required to move to a new Indian territory west of the Mississippi.

Some Indians refused to go. **Black Hawk**, chief of the Sauks, was one of them. In 1832, fighting in Illinois and Wisconsin forced the Sauks out of their homelands forever. Many died; Black Hawk went to prison. The Black Hawk War was just one of many small wars fought between settlers and American Indians.

MANIFEST DESTINY TIMELINE

1783	Treaty of Paris ends Revolutionary War
1803	Louisiana Purchase is made
1820	Missouri Compromise is passed
1836	Texas becomes independent from Mexico
1838	Trail of Tears begins
1845	Texas joins the United States
1846	U.S. and Great Britain agree on Oregon Country boundary; Mexican War begins
1848	Mexican War ends; U.S. receives Mexican Cession; gold discovered in California

The Cherokees of Tennessee and the southeastern United States also refused to leave their homelands. They didn't go to war, however; they went to the Supreme Court of the United States. In a rare victory for American Indians, the Court decided that the Cherokees could keep their homelands. Nevertheless, President Jackson ignored the Court's ruling and forced the Cherokees off their land.

About 4,000 Cherokees died on the 800-mile march to Indian Territory in today's Oklahoma. This march of hunger, thirst, disease, and death became known as the **Trail of Tears**. A Baptist minister who saw the Indians on their journey wrote: "The Cherokees are nearly all prisoners. They have been dragged from their homes . . . [they] were allowed no time to take anything with them except the clothes they had on . . . a painful sight."

Up Close:
New States Join the Union

The treaty that ended the Revolutionary War in 1783 gave the United States the land west of the original 13 states, all the way to the Mississippi River. People had been settling on this land even before independence was won, and it was clear that there would be many new states formed in the area.

The writers of the Constitution could have decided to form colonies in the new American lands, just as the British had formed colonies in North America. They decided instead to make the new states equal to the original 13. When there were enough people in an area to form a government, those people could ask to be added to the Union as a new state. During the years of Manifest Destiny, the United States grew from 13 states to 30.

During the 1850s, people were less interested in Manifest Destiny. The question of whether slavery would be allowed in new states and territories captured the attention of the country. (You'll read about that in Lesson 6.) When the Civil War began in 1861, there were 33 states. During the war, three more would be added.

After the Civil War, Americans began to settle the Great Plains and Rocky Mountain regions, creating states in those areas. The last states, Alaska and Hawaii, joined the Union in 1959, making a total of 50 states.

Will any more states be joining the Union? Some citizens of the District of Columbia and the Caribbean island of Puerto Rico are in favor of statehood. Keep an eye on the news to see if there will be any new stars added to the American flag.

continued on page 37

continued from page 36

New States Join the Union

State	Year		State	Year
Vermont	1791		Oregon	1859
Kentucky	1792		Kansas	1861
Tennessee	1796		West Virginia	1863
Ohio	1803		Nevada	1864
Louisiana	1812		Nebraska	1867
Indiana	1816		Colorado	1876
Mississippi	1817		North Dakota	1889
Illinois	1818		South Dakota	1889
Alabama	1819		Montana	1889
Maine	1820		Washington	1889
Missouri	1821		Idaho	1890
Arkansas	1836		Wyoming	1890
Michigan	1837		Utah	1896
Florida	1845		Oklahoma	1907
Texas	1845		New Mexico	1912
Iowa	1846		Arizona	1912
Wisconsin	1848		Alaska	1959
California	1850		Hawaii	1959
Minnesota	1858			

What Do You Think?

Directions: Answer the questions on the lines provided. Be prepared to discuss your answers in class.

1. The United States and Great Britain settled their differences over Oregon without a war. Why did the United States and Mexico fight a war to settle their differences?

_____

_____

_____

_____

2. If you had been a member of an American Indian tribe in the 1830s, would you have moved peacefully to the Indian Territory? Why or why not?

_____

_____

_____

_____

Test Your Knowledge

Directions: Put the following events into the correct time order. Use "A" for the event that happened first, "B" for the event that happened second, and so on through "G" for the last event. Write the correct letter on the line before each event. Then write the correct year on the line following each event.

_____ 1. Trail of Tears begins _____

_____ 2. Louisiana Purchase is made _____

_____ 3. Lewis & Clark expedition begins _____

_____ 4. Revolutionary War ends _____

_____ 5. Mexican War begins _____

_____ 6. Gold is discovered in California _____

_____ 7. Texas becomes independent _____

Directions: Answer the question on the lines provided.

8. Define "Manifest Destiny."

_____

_____

_____

Lesson 6

One Country, Two Nations

The Louisiana Purchase and Manifest Destiny created a problem for the United States. New territories were added. The question of whether slavery should be allowed in the territories had to be answered. Leaders argued over what the writers of the Constitution wanted to do about slavery. They also argued over what the Declaration of Independence meant when it said "all men are created equal."

Opinions about slavery divided people into three groups. One group, called **abolitionists**, believed that slavery should be stopped immediately and that African Americans should be granted equal rights as citizens. (You'll read more about the abolitionists later in this lesson.) Another group believed that slavery should be allowed where it existed but nowhere else. A third group argued that slaves were property and that people should be allowed to take their property anywhere, even into new territories.

Quick Review 1: What were the three most common opinions about slavery in the United States in the years following the Louisiana Purchase?

_____

_____

_____

New Inventions

In 1793, Eli Whitney invented the **cotton gin**. This machine made it easier to get cotton ready for market. For the first time, profitable cotton plantations spread throughout the South, into the new states of Alabama, Mississippi, and Texas. The plantations needed slaves for cheap labor to plant and harvest the crop.

Two other inventions brought change to American life. The steamboat (1807) and the steam locomotive (about 1830) raised the human speed limit. Now people could travel faster than their own feet or a horse could carry them. More important, large amounts of goods could be transported farther. Both inventions also helped speed movement of settlers to the West. They also helped regions grow. They speeded the growth of business by bringing larger numbers of buyers and settlers together.

IT'S IMPORTANT:

- The question of where slavery should be allowed became very important.

- New inventions and a money economy changed the lives of Americans.

- The Compromise of 1850 was supposed to solve the slavery question.

- Kansas became a battleground over slavery.

- Northerners and Southerners became suspicious of one another for several reasons.

- When Abraham Lincoln, a Republican, was elected president, Southern states left the Union and created the Confederate States of America.

In 1831, Cyrus McCormick of Virginia built the first **mechanical reaper**, a machine for harvesting grain. With a horse-drawn McCormick reaper, a farmer could cut ten acres of grain in a day instead of only one. One farm could now produce more grain with less work. This allowed a farmer to grow grain to sell instead of growing only enough for his family and animals to eat.

Quick Review 2: How did new inventions help the United States to grow?

_____

_____

_____

COMPROMISE AND CONFLICT TIMELINE

1820	Missouri Compromise is passed by Congress
1850	Compromise of 1850 is passed
1854	Kansas-Nebraska Act is passed
1856	People opposed to Kansas-Nebraska Act form Republican party
1857	Supreme Court announces Dred Scott decision
1858	Lincoln-Douglas debates held in Illinois
1860	Abraham Lincoln elected president; Southern states form Confederacy

Money and the New Nation

The United States quickly grew into a nation of regions. The Northeast became a manufacturing region, thanks to new machines and people to run them. The Southern states became a plantation society with slave labor and farms growing only one crop, such as cotton or tobacco. The western borders of the expanding nation, today's Midwest, grew grains and livestock on small farms.

Money was not always important to all Americans. On the expanding frontier, the barter economy was alive and well. A person might trade a butchered hog for a doctor's services or some hours of labor for a sack of flour.

As the country grew, transportation improved, and regions began trading with one another. Products from Northern factories moved to the South and the West in exchange for harvests grown in those areas. Products from Europe came across the ocean to trade for products made in America. Suddenly, barter didn't work as well.

The United States moved toward a money economy. Working people traded their labor for wages. Farmers traded their harvests for money. A system of **credit** (money lent now to be paid back later) was important to economic growth. Bankers lent money to farmers and merchants and expected interest in return. A strong banking system kept the economy afloat. The U.S. Treasury printed the money, which was backed by silver and gold.

Quick Review 3: What shifted the United States toward an economy based on money and credit?

_____

_____

_____

_____

_____

Different Views Toward Slavery

It's not correct to say that all Northern people were abolitionists and that all Southerners were slaveholders. The reality is more complicated.

- Abolitionism was unpopular in the North as well as the South. Many Northerners who believed that slavery was wrong did not believe that African Americans were entitled to equal rights.

- Seventy-five percent of all Southerners owned no slaves. Yet many of these Southerners supported slavery. They either hoped to become slaveholders or they believed that African Americans were inferior and belonged in slavery.

- Some Southern slaveholders were against the idea of slavery, but they believed it was the only way for them to run their farms and make a living.

- Many antislavery people in both the North and South believed that freed slaves should go back to Africa. African American leaders, who were Northern citizens known as **free blacks**, opposed this. They considered the United States to be their home.

- Some Southerners argued that slavery was good for African Americans and that Northerners should consider enslaving their lower classes of people.

Up Close:
Calhoun, Webster, and Clay

During the middle of the 1800s, three of the most important men in the United States Senate were John C. Calhoun of South Carolina, Daniel Webster of Massachusetts, and Henry Clay of Kentucky.

Calhoun stood for states' rights. He believed that the Constitution protected states from the powerful national government. He strongly supported the South's agricultural way of life, including slavery.

> *May we all remember that [the Union] can only be preserved by respecting the rights of the states . . .*
>
> —**John C. Calhoun**, 1830

Webster was a Boston lawyer famous for his speaking skills. Unlike Calhoun, he believed in a strong national government. He wanted to see special taxes called **tariffs** used to protect Northern industries. (Calhoun believed tariffs hurt farmers.) Webster was against the spread of slavery.

> *Liberty and Union, now and forever, one and inseparable.*
>
> —**Daniel Webster**, 1830

Henry Clay's views fell between those of Calhoun and Webster. Clay was "the Great Compromiser." He tried to bridge the differences between those who shared the views of Calhoun and Webster. Clay pushed both the Missouri Compromise and the Compromise of 1850. He believed that the national government could unite the regions by building roads and bridges and running a national bank. He called his idea "the American system."

> *I know no South, no North, no East, no West. . . . the Union, sir, is my country.*
>
> —**Henry Clay**, 1848

Each man wanted to become president. Clay ran five times and never won. Calhoun had to quit as vice president because he disagreed with President Andrew Jackson. Webster deeply regretted his failure to become president.

The Missouri Compromise (1820)

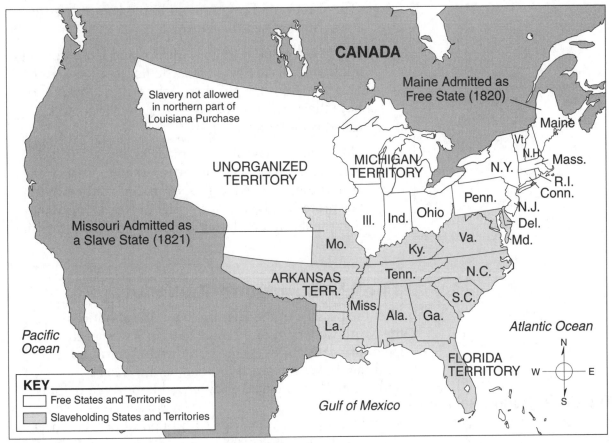

Trouble

In 1820, the United States hit the first bump on the road of westward expansion. Slavery was legal. Most of the Northern states chose to abolish it, but it was still widespread in the South. Antislavery people wanted to keep slavery out of new territories. Pro-slavery people wanted it there.

The **Missouri Compromise** resolved the disagreement. Missouri joined the United States; slavery was allowed there. Maine joined at the same time. It was a free (non-slavery) state. Congress decided that slavery would be allowed in any states south of a line drawn across the new territory along the southern border of Missouri.

Compromise of 1850

The Missouri Compromise was supposed to solve the slavery problem forever. It didn't. When the United States added new territory in 1848, after the Mexican War, the South wanted slavery to be allowed there. It took another compromise to settle the question.

The **Compromise of 1850** had three major parts:

- California would be admitted to the Union as a free state. This pleased the North.

- The new territories of New Mexico and Utah would be allowed to decide by a vote whether to allow slavery. This gave both the North and the South a chance to have their way. The idea of voting on slavery was called **popular sovereignty**.

- The **Fugitive Slave Act** was made stronger. The law required escaped slaves to be returned to their owners, even if they escaped to the North. Southerners felt the law protected their property rights. Northerners said that the law made slavery national, not just something Southern.

The Underground Railroad

After the passage of the Fugitive Slave Act, abolitionists in the North were even more eager to help slaves reach freedom. Many slaves escaped on the **Underground Railroad**. It was not a real railroad, and it wasn't underground. It operated aboveground, in secret, helping slaves flee across fields, through woods, and over rivers. Like a real railroad, it had stations, conductors, and passengers. The "passengers" were runaway slaves; the "conductors" were guides; the "stations" were hiding places. Its goal was to get slaves to the free states or to Canada, beyond the reach of slave-catchers.

Underground Railroad stations were houses, barns, churches, stores, and schoolhouses. "Stationmasters" provided runaways with shelter and food. Stationmasters were ordinary people, such as farmers, merchants, and ministers. They shared a belief that slavery was wrong, and they wanted to help African Americans escape bondage.

The Underground Railroad

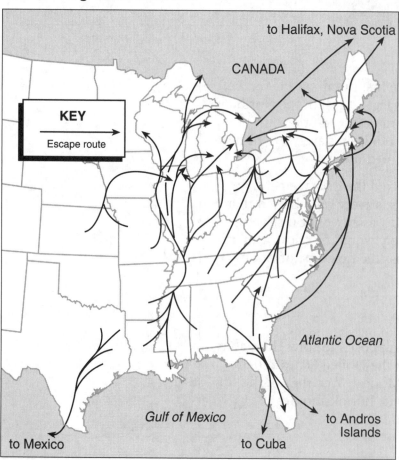

Conductors guided runaway slaves from one station to another. The conductors had to be brave, because the Underground Railroad was dangerous. Prison, slavery, or even death awaited anyone caught working on this railroad.

Harriet Tubman was the most famous conductor on the Underground Railroad. She was born a slave in Maryland around 1820. Whippings left her scarred and a head injury left her in ill health, but in 1849 she escaped from slavery. A year later, she made her first trip south to guide slaves to freedom. In all, Tubman made 19 trips on the railroad. In 1857, she helped her mother and father escape. Southern slaveholders offered a reward of $40,000 for anyone who could capture her, but no one did. Tubman never lost a slave on any of her trips.

The Underground Railroad carried thousands of slaves along its dangerous routes to freedom. It operated until 1865, when slavery was ended by the Thirteenth Amendment to the Constitution.

Quick Review 4: What was the purpose of the Underground Railroad?

_____

_____

_____

Kansas Explodes

After the Compromise of 1850, the next challenge was what to do about the territories of Kansas and Nebraska. According to the Missouri Compromise, slavery was not allowed there. In 1854, Illinois senator **Stephen A. Douglas** proposed the **Kansas-Nebraska Act**. This act would allow these territories to decide on slavery based on popular sovereignty. Congress voted in favor of it. This sent pro- and antislavery people pouring into Kansas. They fought bloody battles trying to gain control of the territory, which became known as "bleeding Kansas."

Some opponents of the Kansas-Nebraska Act formed a new party, the **Republicans**. In their first election in 1856, the Republicans won many votes in the free states, but a Democrat, James Buchanan, was elected president. The other major U.S. party, the Whigs, disappeared from history.

The Dred Scott Decision

In 1857, the Supreme Court ruled on the case of **Dred Scott**, a slave who had lived in free territory for several years. Scott argued that living in an area where slavery was illegal made him a free man. The Court disagreed. They said that Scott was not free, and that African Americans had no rights as citizens. The Court ruled that slaves were property and that people had the right to take their property anywhere in the United States, even into new territories.

The Dred Scott decision made Northerners believe their worst fears were coming true. All of the compromises were declared illegal. It was possible that the Northern states might be forced to permit slavery.

It Wasn't Just Slavery . . .

The conflicts between the North and the South were not only over slavery. Between 1820 and 1860, the two sections grew apart in other ways.

The **Industrial Revolution** came to the North during these years. Factories were built to make goods faster and cheaper than ever before. Railroads made it easier to transport and sell products far away from where they were made. Because large amounts of money were needed to create new industries, banking became a big business in the North. Cities grew as people came to them looking for factory jobs.

The Southern economy was based on farms, not factories. The South had only 30 percent of the nation's railroads and 15 percent of its factories. There were fewer large cities. Most people lived in the country.

Southerners distrusted the national government. They believed it favored the North over the South. Southerners thought the states should have the greatest control over the lives of their citizens.

Northerners and Southerners had one thing in common: Each group believed that it was following in the footsteps of Washington, Jefferson, and Franklin, and that the other group had gone wrong.

James Buchanan

President James Buchanan, a native of Pennsylvania, believed slavery was wrong but that the Constitution protected it. He also believed that states had no right to leave the Union but that the Constitution contained nothing that could stop them.

Quick Review 5: List two ways in which the South and North were different in the years before 1860.

_____

_____

The Break

In 1858, the entire United States followed the campaign for U.S. Senator in Illinois. One candidate was Stephen A. Douglas, the Democrat who wrote the Kansas-Nebraska Act. The other was **Abraham Lincoln**, a Republican who opposed the spread of slavery. The two argued the slavery issue in seven famous debates held around the state. Lincoln lost the election, but he became the leading Republican spokesman against the spread of slavery.

In 1860, the Republicans nominated Lincoln for president. The Democrats were divided and had two candidates. Douglas was one of them, but he ran only in the North. As a result of the split, Lincoln was elected president with no support from the South. Southerners were now sure that slavery would be abolished.

For more than 30 years, some Southerners had insisted that the South had the right to leave the United States and form its own union. Six weeks after Lincoln's election, South Carolina decided to **secede** (separate; pronounced *sih-SEED*). Over the next few weeks, Alabama, Florida, Mississippi, Georgia, Louisiana, and Texas followed. Together they formed the **Confederate States of America**. **Jefferson Davis** of Mississippi became their president.

President James Buchanan was still in charge during the first two months of 1861, but he did nothing to help settle the crisis. Lincoln was sworn in on March 4th. No one in the North or the South knew exactly what might come next.

What Do You Think?

Directions: Answer the questions on the lines provided. Be prepared to discuss your answers in class.

1. What was the biggest cause of the Civil War? Give reasons why you think so.

_____

_____

_____

_____

_____

_____

2. Did the Southern states have the right to leave the Union? Why or why not?

_____

_____

_____

_____

_____

Test Your Knowledge

Directions: Put the events listed into correct order on the timeline. Write the letter of the event next to the correct year. Not all the spaces on the timeline will be used.

A. Kansas-Nebraska Act

B. Southern states secede from the Union

C. Republican party's first election

D. Lincoln elected president

E. Compromise of 1850

F. Lincoln-Douglas debates

G. Dred Scott decision

1850	_____
1851	_____
1852	_____
1853	_____
1854	_____
1855	_____
1856	_____
1857	_____
1858	_____
1859	_____
1860	_____
1861	_____

Directions: Fill in the blank with the word or words that complete each sentence correctly.

1. _____ were people who demanded that slavery should be ended immediately.

2. Because of the _____, factories and businesses were growing rapidly in the North, but the South fell behind.

3. The plan that put California into the Union and included the Fugitive Slave Act was

   called the_____ of 1850.

4. The _____ was a network of stations and conductors

   that helped slaves escape from the South.

5. The 1854 law that permitted two territories to vote on whether they wanted slavery or

   not was called the _____ Act.

6. The new _____ party was made up of people opposed to slavery.

7. The court case that said African Americans were not citizens and that Southerners could

   take their property anywhere was the _____ decision.

8. In 1858, debates were held between Abraham _____ and

   Stephen _____, who were running for U.S. Senator in Illinois.

9. When Abraham Lincoln was elected, some Southern states decided to

   _____ from the Union.

10. In 1861, the Southern states formed the _____ of America.

Lesson 7

The Civil War

By April 12, 1861, seven states had already left the United States of America to form the Confederacy. U.S. troops still held a few forts in Confederate territory. One of them was **Fort Sumter**, in the harbor of Charleston, South Carolina. When the U.S. government tried to deliver supplies to its soldiers at Fort Sumter, Confederate soldiers fired on the fort. The Civil War had begun.

The action at Fort Sumter had two important effects:

- Virginia, North Carolina, Tennessee, and Arkansas joined the Confederacy.

- The Northern states united in an effort to keep the Union together. Lincoln called for volunteer soldiers to serve in the army and stop the rebellion.

IT'S IMPORTANT:

- The Civil War began when the Confederates fired on Fort Sumter in Charleston, S.C.

- Important fighting happened between Richmond, Virginia, and Washington, D.C., and along the Mississippi River.

- The war brought hardship to soldiers and people at home on both sides.

- Bloody battles raged for four years.

- Abraham Lincoln announced the Emancipation Proclamation freeing the slaves in 1862.

Bull Run

At the beginning, both sides believed that the war wouldn't be a long one. Confederates believed the Union army would run away when the first battle was fought. The North believed their army would quickly destroy the rebels. On July 21, 1861, the two sides met for the first big battle of the war, near Washington, D.C.

People rode out from Washington to watch the battle. It was a Sunday, and they brought picnic lunches. Many spectators were caught in the retreat when the battle turned out to be a bloody defeat for the Union army. After the battle (called **Bull Run** by the Union and **Manassas** by the Confederacy), neither side talked about a quick war anymore. (Later, this battle would be called "First Bull Run" and "First Manassas," after a second battle was fought at the same place.)

Americans at War

Much of the fighting in the Civil War happened in Virginia, between Washington, D.C., and Richmond, Virginia, the Confederate capital. The two cities were only 90 miles apart. The main goal of both sides was to capture the other's capital city.

Hundreds of miles away, another Union goal was to control the Mississippi River. Rivers were used for transporting soldiers and supplies, so control of them was very important to both sides. If the Union could take the Mississippi, the Confederacy would be divided in two and might be defeated more easily.

A major Confederate goal was simply to hang on. The Confederates did not have to wipe out the Union army to win their independence. Confederate leaders hoped to make the war last as long as possible. The longer it lasted, the better the chances that the Northern people would demand an end to the war and let the Confederacy become independent.

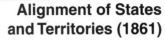

Alignment of States and Territories (1861)

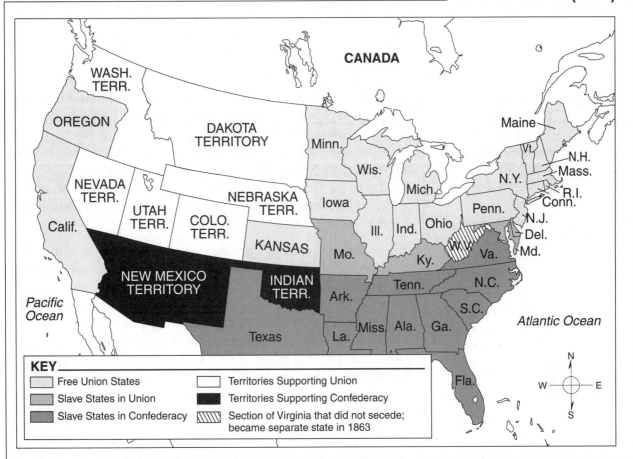

KEY

Free Union States	Territories Supporting Union
Slave States in Union	Territories Supporting Confederacy
Slave States in Confederacy	Section of Virginia that did not secede; became separate state in 1863

Above: *American states and territories were lined up this way at the start of the Civil War in 1861.*

Quick Review 1: What two things did the Union want to do in order to beat the Confederacy?

_____

_____

How did the Confederacy believe it could win its independence?

_____

_____

Life on the Battlefield

Thousands of young men were happy to enlist in the Union and Confederate armies. The biggest fear of many was that the war would be over before they could get into a battle. After living through one battle, however, soldiers learned that war was not what they expected.

Major battles were terrifying: loud and smoky with soldiers being shot to death, blown up, or terribly hurt all around. It was considered shameful to show fear, but almost every soldier was afraid some of the time.

One of every four Civil War soldiers was killed or wounded. Wounded soldiers would sometimes lie on the battlefield for hours or days before help arrived. Even then, help might not do much good. Medical knowledge was limited. For example, the cure for a serious gunshot wound in an arm or leg was to cut off the arm or leg. Doctors' tools and bandages were often unsanitary. As a result, wounds became infected, but doctors didn't understand why. There were few drugs to ease pain.

When armies were not fighting or marching, they spent time in camp. Camp life also could be dangerous. Diseases were easily caught and spread. (More men died of disease in the Civil War than in battle.) Camp life was boring, too. Some units passed the time by marching and practicing with their weapons. Otherwise, men spent their time reading, playing cards, writing or reading letters, and sometimes getting into trouble. Fistfights and drunkenness were not unusual. Often, soldiers welcomed battle simply to have something new to do.

Union soldiers were better-fed than Confederates, thanks to the Union states' ability to produce more food. Soldiers on both sides often ate **hardtack**, a flat bread that could break a man's teeth unless he softened it in his coffee first. (Coffee was the favorite beverage of both sides, although it was very hard to get in the Confederate army.) The best source of meat was whatever the soldiers could find in the countryside. The army provided some meat, but it often wasn't very good. **Salt pork**, which was very much like bacon, was often on the army menu.

Union soldiers sometimes got dried vegetable cakes, which were supposed to be made into soup. (Some of the vegetable cakes had been made during the Mexican War, which ended in 1848.) A soldier who received a food package from home was a very lucky man.

CIVIL WAR TIMELINE

1860	Lincoln elected president of the United States; Confederacy is formed
1861	April: Confederates fire on Fort Sumter in Charleston, S.C.; more Southern states join the Confederacy
1861	July: Battle of Bull Run/Manassas is the first big battle of the war
1862	April: Union and Confederate troops clash in the battle of Shiloh
1862	September: More men are killed and wounded at the Battle of Antietam than at any other American battle; Lincoln announces Emancipation Proclamation
1863	July: Union wins battles of Gettysburg and Vicksburg on the same day
1865	April: Confederate army runs out of men and supplies; their surrender ends the war

Life on the Homefront

Very few families were untouched by the Civil War. If a family member was not in the army, a friend of the family probably was. Those at home waited eagerly for letters. They also read the papers for war news. Newspapers printed lists of soldiers killed in battle; sometimes this was how families learned about the death of a loved one.

Women helped with the war effort. They made bandages and collected supplies for the armies. They held fairs and exhibits to raise money for hospitals. Some women volunteered to serve as nurses. Others whose husbands joined the armies were left to manage farms and businesses. They proved that they were able to do many of the same things men did.

Civilians (non-army people) of the South felt the war more directly than civilians of the North. Northern farms and factories kept producing food and needed goods. The South was less able to produce what it needed and had to buy it. The Northern navy kept Southern ports from receiving shipments; therefore, some goods were hard to find and high priced. As the war went on, food and supplies were sent to the armies instead of being sold to civilians. In 1863, Richmond was shaken by food riots as hungry people demanded that the government feed them. By war's end, a bag of flour cost hundreds of dollars.

The Southern people also had to live with armies in their territory. Soldiers from both sides simply took what they needed. They cut down trees for firewood and killed animals for food even though their commanders ordered them not to. When battles broke out, small towns and farms were often caught in the middle. The town of Winchester, Virginia, went back and forth between the Union and the Confederacy. It was captured by one army or the other 130 times.

Wilmer McLean

The battle of Bull Run, the first big battle of the war, was fought on and around Wilmer McLean's farm near Manassas, Virginia. Afterward, McLean decided to move his family to a quieter place. He chose a small Virginia crossroads named Appomattox Court House. In 1865, Robert E. Lee met Ulysses S. Grant to surrender his army and end the war. The place they chose to meet was Wilmer McLean's house.

Four Years of Fighting

The Civil War was fought all across the United States, from Florida to Vermont to the New Mexico Territory. There was even an ocean battle near Great Britain. There were hundreds of small fights and many large battles. In addition to Bull Run, other famous battles were fought at **Shiloh**, along the border between Mississippi and Tennessee; along **Antietam** Creek near Sharpsburg, Maryland; at **Gettysburg**, Pennsylvania; at **Chancellorsville**, Virginia; and around **Chattanooga**, Tennessee.

At the time the battle of Shiloh was fought, it was the bloodiest battle in American history, although future battles would see even more men killed and wounded. At Chancellorsville, the great Confederate general, **Stonewall Jackson**, was accidentally killed by his own men. The three-day battle of Gettysburg, won by the Union, is the most famous battle of the war. Another Union army won control of the Mississippi River at **Vicksburg**, Mississippi, on the same day, July 3, 1863. The Confederacy never had a real chance to win the war after that day.

Confederate armies fought well and had better leaders but were unable to hang on against the Union. As the years went by, the North's stronger economy and larger population made the difference. In early 1865, a Northern army led by **William T. Sherman** marched through the South, destroying towns and farms. In April, the weakened Confederates were forced out of their capital city, Richmond. A few days later, Confederate General **Robert E. Lee** surrendered to Union general **Ulysses S. Grant** at Appomattox, Virginia. The Civil War came to an end.

Quick Review 2: Give the importance of each battle listed.

Bull Run: _____

_____

Chancellorsville: _____

_____

Vicksburg: _____

_____

"Forever Free"

When the Civil War began, not even Abraham Lincoln thought it was a war to end slavery. Lincoln and most of the North believed the war was being fought to keep the Union together.

In 1862, the war was not going well for the North. Lincoln decided that he had to do something serious to harm the Southern war effort. He also wanted to keep European countries from helping the Confederacy. In September, Lincoln announced the **Emancipation Proclamation**, which declared that all slaves in areas rebelling against the United States were to be "forever free." It was to go into effect on January 1, 1863.

The Emancipation Proclamation did not free slaves in the border states or in parts of the Confederacy controlled by Union troops. It applied only to slaves in areas that did not accept the United States government! (Therefore, some historians say that it really didn't free anybody.) Lincoln did not believe he had the right to free all the slaves everywhere without amending the Constitution.

The Proclamation kept European countries from helping the South by turning the war into a fight for human freedom. It was opposed by many Northerners, who were happy to fight for the Union but did not want to fight to free African Americans.

If I could save the Union without freeing any slave, I would do it; if I could save it by freeing all the slaves, I would do it; and if I could do it by freeing some and leaving others alone, I would also do that.

—**Abraham Lincoln**, 1862

The Emancipation Proclamation also made it clear that if the North won the war, the lives of African Americans would be forever changed. It permitted African Americans to enlist in the Union army. More than 180,000 of them did. Although they faced discrimination and were paid less than white soldiers, they welcomed the chance to fight for freedom.

Quick Review 3: What did the Emancipation Proclamation do?

_____

_____

_____

_____

What did the Emancipation Proclamation not do?

_____

_____

_____

_____

End of the War and After

The North had more people and bigger industries than the South. This meant that the North had more resources to fight the Civil War. In the end, those resources won out. Starting late in 1864, Confederate armies in Virginia and elsewhere in the South were always low on supplies. Many Confederate soldiers simply went home to defend their families personally. In the end, Lee surrendered to Grant.

The end of the war brought great joy in the North. The Union had been saved. In the South, countless lives had been changed by the death and destruction the war brought to their region. They understood that their way of life would never again be the way it was before the war.

The Meaning of the War

Abraham Lincoln thought long and hard about the meaning of the Civil War. In his most famous speech, the **Gettysburg Address**, he tried to explain it. On November 19, 1863, at the dedication of a cemetery for soldiers who died at the battle of Gettysburg, Lincoln said:

"Four score and seven years ago, our fathers brought forth upon this continent a new nation: conceived in liberty, and dedicated to the proposition that all men are created equal. Now we are engaged in a great civil war, testing whether that nation, or any nation so conceived and so dedicated, can long endure. We are met on a great battlefield of that war. We have come to dedicate a portion of that field as a final resting place for those who here gave their lives that this nation might live. It is altogether fitting and proper that we should do this."

Lincoln explains that in 1776, the United States was created, based on the ideas of freedom and equality. Eighty-seven years later, the Civil War tests whether a nation built on those ideas can survive. Americans meet on this day to honor the soldiers who died defending freedom and equality.

"But in a larger sense, we cannot dedicate; we cannot consecrate; we cannot hallow this ground. The brave men, living and dead, who struggled here have consecrated it, far above our poor power to add or detract. The world will little note nor long remember what we say here, but it can never forget what they did here."

The Surrender

Lee's surrender of his army, on April 9, 1865, ended the war, but it was not the last surrender of the war. An even larger Confederate army surrendered in North Carolina in May. A force led by General Stand Watie, a three-quarter Cherokee, hung on west of the Mississippi until June. The last Confederate navy ship to surrender didn't give up until November, seven months after Lee met Grant at Appomattox.

Lincoln says that the soldiers who fought and died have done more to honor the Gettysburg cemetery than any living person can do. Although his speech will not be remembered (or so he thought), the soldiers will never be forgotten.

"It is for us the living, rather, to be here dedicated to the unfinished work which they who fought here have thus far so nobly advanced. It is rather for us to be here dedicated to the great task remaining before us; that from these honored dead we take increased devotion to the cause for which they gave the last full measure of devotion; that we here highly resolve that these dead shall not have died in vain . . ."

Our job, Lincoln says, is to do the work the soldiers began. Their willingness to die should make us willing to work even harder.

"[We must resolve] that this nation, under God, shall have a new birth of freedom; and that government of the people, by the people, for the people, shall not perish from the earth."

Quick Review 4: What does Lincoln mean in the last lines of the Gettysburg Address?

_____

_____

_____

_____

What Do You Think?

Directions: Answer the questions on the lines provided. Be prepared to discuss your answers in class.

1. In some Civil War battles, thousands of soldiers were killed and wounded in a single day. Why did people of the North and South allow so much bloodshed during the Civil War?

_____

_____

_____

2. What if the Confederacy had won the war? How would our lives be different?

_____

_____

_____

Test Your Knowledge

Directions: Fill in the blanks in the clues, then find the words in the puzzle. All words go only from left to right and up to down; none are spelled backwards or diagonally.

1. The Civil War started when the Confederates fired on Fort _____.

2. In 1862, President _____ announced the Emancipation Proclamation.

3. Two battles were fought at a place called _____.

4. General Stand _____ led Native American troops.

5. The battle of Antietam was fought near the town of _____, Maryland.

6. The Union won the battle of _____ on the same day as the battle of Gettysburg.

7. Confederate troops were led by Robert E. _____.

8. The Confederate capital city was _____, Virginia.

9. Union general William T. _____ marched through the South.

10. The battle of _____ was fought in Pennsylvania on July 1, 2, and 3, 1863.

11. The Union commander at the end of the Civil War was General Ulysses S. _____.

12. Confederate hero Stonewall _____ was killed at Chancellorsville.

13. The capital city of the Union was _____, D.C.

14. In April of 1862, the battle of _____ was the bloodiest ever up to that time.

15. General Lee surrendered to General Grant at _____.

S	H	A	R	P	S	B	U	R	G	W	S
U	A	M	N	R	O	U	Y	C	B	A	H
M	P	V	B	I	A	L	Z	J	W	S	E
T	L	I	N	C	O	L	N	I	A	H	R
E	K	C	C	H	G	R	A	N	T	I	M
R	M	K	O	M	W	U	U	H	I	N	A
X	O	S	F	O	V	N	L	E	E	G	N
T	Q	B	E	N	D	S	T	G	F	T	D
S	I	U	Q	D	R	S	H	I	L	O	H
V	L	R	H	J	A	C	K	S	O	N	E
K	G	G	E	T	T	Y	S	B	U	R	G
A	P	P	O	M	A	T	T	O	X	C	H

Lesson 8

Reconstruction

The period of time following the Civil War is known as **Reconstruction**. Abraham Lincoln wanted to bring the Southern states back into the Union quickly and peacefully, but he didn't live to see it happen. On April 14, 1865, only five days after the Confederate surrender, Lincoln was assassinated by **John Wilkes Booth**, a well-known actor who supported the Confederacy.

Putting the Union Back Together

Lincoln's vice president, **Andrew Johnson**, tried to carry out Lincoln's reconstruction plan, but he was unsuccessful. Republicans in Congress wanted to punish the South for the Civil War, and they were powerful enough to see their wishes carried out. Three amendments were added to the Constitution to end slavery and to give African Americans legal rights, and, later, the right to vote. Southern states were not allowed back into the Union until they approved these amendments. Soldiers were sent into the South to see that freed slaves received their legal rights.

Former Confederate officials were not allowed to vote. African Americans were, and they elected several former slaves to leadership positions. **Hiram Revels** and **Blanche K. Bruce** represented Mississippi in the United States Senate. There were several African Americans elected to the House of Representatives.

As time passed after the war, former Confederates were given back their voting rights. They slowly regained control of state governments in the South. African Americans lost many of the rights they enjoyed in the early years of Reconstruction. Northerners became less interested in Reconstruction. In 1877, the newly elected president, **Rutherford B. Hayes**, agreed to remove the soldiers from the South. Reconstruction was over.

IT'S IMPORTANT:

- Republicans in Congress wanted to punish the South with a tough Reconstruction plan.

- Freed slaves gained and lost rights during Reconstruction.

- Three amendments to the Constitution were written to give legal rights to African Americans.

- Reconstruction helped rebuild the South but mostly failed in giving equal rights to the former slaves.

Quick Review 1: What did African Americans gain during Reconstruction?

_____

_____

What did they lose at the end of Reconstruction?

_____

_____

Reconstruction Amendments

Abraham Lincoln's Emancipation Proclamation had ended slavery only in places rebelling against the United States. Once the rebellion was over, slavery would still be legal unless the Constitution was changed. In January of 1865, before the Civil War ended, Congress passed an amendment outlawing slavery. It was ratified in December of the same year. It became the **Thirteenth Amendment**.

The Constitution did not define "citizenship." In 1857, before the Civil War began, the Supreme Court's Dred Scott decision had ruled that blacks were not citizens of the United States. To defend the rights of blacks, Congress wrote a definition of citizenship and put it into the **Fourteenth Amendment**, which was ratified in 1868. It said that anyone born in the United States was a citizen.

The Fourteenth Amendment also promised every citizen "equal protection under the law." It said that no state could take away "life, liberty, or property without due process of law." The amendment was intended to stop discrimination and give basic rights to freed slaves. It also would punish states that denied voting rights to citizens by taking away representatives in Congress. No state was ever punished in this way, however.

The Fourteenth Amendment did not mention black voting rights directly. The **Fifteenth Amendment** did. It gave the right to vote to all citizens of any race, color, or "previous condition of servitude"—in other words, to former slaves. Even in the North, black voting rights were sometimes limited. Therefore, the Fifteenth Amendment was aimed at both Northern and Southern states. It was ratified in 1870.

Quick Review 2: Briefly explain the purpose of each amendment.

Thirteenth: _____

_____

Fourteenth: _____

_____

_____

Fifteenth: _____

_____

The Effect

After the Civil War and Reconstruction, the Industrial Revolution came to the South. New railroad lines were built to replace the ones destroyed during the war and to bring railroad service to areas that had never had it. Cities and factories grew as they had done in the North 30 years before. Most of this growth came thanks to Northern businessmen, who invested their money in the South.

Mistrust between the North and South didn't end with the war. Most Southerners hated the Northerners who came to the South to help the freed slaves or invest money. Northerners didn't always believe the Southern people were glad to be back in the Union.

Although the Industrial Revolution brought changes, the South remained an agricultural area. Four million freed slaves needed to support their families and, for many, farming was all they knew. Most of them were too poor to buy land, tools, and seed of their own. A system developed called **sharecropping**. Freed slaves (and many poor white Southerners) worked on land owned by someone else. In exchange for use of the land, the sharecropper gave part of the crop he raised to the owner of the land. If the crop failed, the sharecropper might owe twice as much to the owner the next year. For many, sharecropping wasn't much different from slavery.

Much of the South was badly damaged by the war. Towns, homes, and farms were wiped out. Many people, black and white, slipped into poverty.

When the North lost interest in Reconstruction, Southern states moved quickly to restrict the civil rights of the freed slaves. States passed laws making it difficult or impossible for former slaves to vote. Those who still tried were sometimes harassed or killed by the **Ku Klux Klan**, a terrorist organization. Laws were passed setting up separate schools, train cars, and even public drinking fountains for black and white people. In 1896, the Supreme Court ruled that as long as public facilities like these were equal, they could be separate.

The separation of races in the South would not begin to change until the Civil Rights Movement of the 1950s and 1960s. The hatreds of that time re-opened many of the wounds of the Civil War. As we head into the 21st century, some of those wounds still hurt the United States. Much of the mistrust between black and white Americans today has its roots in the period of the Civil War and Reconstruction.

Quick Review 3: Name three effects of the Civil War and Reconstruction.

_____

_____

_____

_____

What Do You Think?

Directions: Answer the question on the lines provided. Be prepared to discuss your answer in class.

Reconstruction created lasting mistrust between the North and the South. Why did this happen?

_____

_____

_____

_____

_____

Test Your Knowledge

Directions: Answer the questions on the lines provided.

1. The three "Reconstruction amendments" to the Constitution were written to do three things for African Americans. What were they?

_____

_____

_____

_____

_____

2. How did Reconstruction bring the Industrial Revolution to the South?

_____

_____

_____

_____

_____

3. What happened to the rights of former slaves in the South after 1877? Why did this happen?

_____

_____

_____

_____

_____

Unit I Review Test

1. Which Indian nation formed a League of Five Nations to work together for peace?

   A. Inuits   C. Iroquois
   B. Anasazi   D. Kwakiutls

2. By the 1880s, buffalo populations on the Great Plains, which had once numbered in the millions, had fallen to about 1,000. What happened?

   A. Disease struck the buffalo population, killing them.

   B. Increasing numbers of Indians hunted more buffalo.

   C. The buffalo were no longer useful to the Indians of the Plains.

   D. Thousands were killed by white hunters for their skins.

3. What was one way in which geography influenced the Inuits?

   A. They built homes on and near the sides of cliffs.

   B. They drained a swamp to build their capital city.

   C. They developed technology that helped them live in the cold.

   D. They built a large network of roads to help rule their empire.

4. If you were a follower of the Puritan religion who lived in a town but farmed on land outside of town, you most likely lived in

   A. Virginia.   C. Pennsylvania.
   B. Maryland.   D. Massachusetts.

Explorers: Who and Why

5. Which explorer traveled up the St. Lawrence River into Canada?

   A. John Cabot
   B. Jacques Cartier
   C. Hernando DeSoto
   D. Christopher Columbus

6. Which item listed below was not a major reason why Europeans explored and built colonies in the New World?

   A. start profit-making businesses

   B. convert native people to Christianity

   C. increase the wealth and power of their countries

   D. make more room in overcrowded European cities

7. The British government first began putting taxes on the American colonies because

   A. King George III and Parliament were greedy.

   B. Great Britain wanted to punish Boston for destroying tea.

   C. Great Britain wanted a share of American trade profits.

   D. Parliament wanted America to share the cost of the French and Indian War.

8. When the British marched on Lexington and Concord in April of 1775, they were looking for

   A. John Adams and Patrick Henry.

   B. John Hancock and Samuel Adams.

   C. Thomas Jefferson and Benjamin Franklin.

   D. George Washington and the Continental Army.

9. In addition to becoming a free country, what else did the United States get from the British at the end of the Revolutionary War?

   A. British land from the Atlantic to the Mississippi River

   B. money to pay for damage to American homes

   C. British land in Europe and Africa

   D. the right to sell tea in British cities

10. "I think that what this country needs is a strong national government. I said that when we were deciding on the Constitution a few years ago, and I say it again right now. We need a national bank! Who am I?"

    A. a loyalist

    B. a Federalist

    C. a Republican

    D. an Anti-Federalist

Directions: Look at the picture, then use it to answer Numbers 11 and 12.

Lewis and Clark Expedition

11. Sacagawea was most helpful to Lewis and Clark because

    A. she had guided many settlers across the continent.

    B. like many Indian women, she was an experienced hunter.

    C. she knew much of the territory and could speak another language.

    D. they needed to have an Indian along to help raise money on the trip.

12. Lewis and Clark were exploring Montana because

    A. the territory was part of the Louisiana Purchase.

    B. the United States had won the territory in the Mexican War.

    C. they were scouting for the Continental Army in the Revolutionary War.

    D. it was located on the way to Oregon, which Britain hired them to explore.

Above: *Sacagawea, the American Indian woman who traveled with Lewis and Clark*

---

13. The defense of the Alamo by Texas soldiers happened

    A. between the Missouri Compromise and the Civil War.

    B. between the Compromise of 1850 and Reconstruction.

    C. between the Louisiana Purchase and the War of 1812.

    D. between the signing of the Constitution and the Louisiana Purchase.

Directions: Look at the map, then use it to answer Numbers 14 and 15.

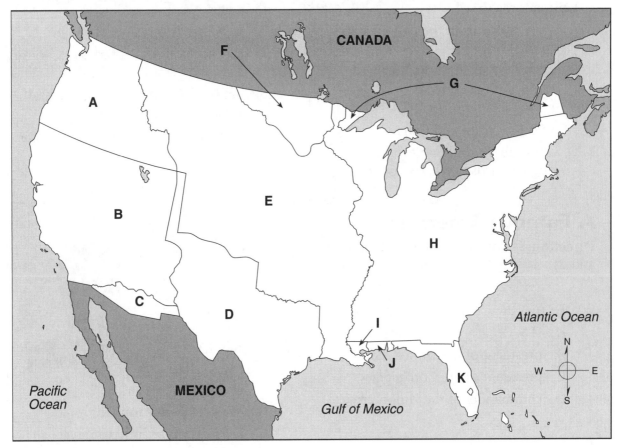

14. Which area on the map is the Oregon Country?

    A. A   C. C

    B. B   D. D

15. Which area on the map became part of the United States after the Mexican War?

    A. A   C. E

    B. B   D. K

Directions: Read the statement, then use it to answer Number 16.

Now that it's the year 1855, I want to move to Kansas. If I can take my tools and my farm animals with me, I should be able take my slaves, too. I don't believe the government of the United States has any right to tell me what I can do with my property.

16. The person making this statement is most likely a

    A. Northerner.   C. abolitionist.

    B. Southerner.   D. Republican.

17. Many Northern people hated the Fugitive Slave Act because it

    A. required that slaves be returned, even if they escaped to the North.

    B. overturned all laws making slavery illegal in the Northern states.

    C. made popular sovereignty legal in the Kansas and Nebraska territories.

    D. caused large numbers of African Americans to come to Northern cities.

18. The purpose of the Underground Railroad was to

    A. carry goods from the eastern states to the West.

    B. carry tourists from the northern states to the South.

    C. help slaves escape from the South into the North and Canada.

    D. allow abolitionists to escape from angry crowds of slavery supporters.

19. Most of the fighting in the Civil War took place

    A. in Pennsylvania and Maryland.

    B. at Fort Sumter in Charleston, South Carolina.

    C. between Richmond, Virginia, and Washington, D.C.

    D. along the Mississippi River from St. Louis to New Orleans.

A Famous American

Directions: Look at the picture, then use it to answer Numbers 20 and 21.

20. During the Civil War, this man was

    A. U.S. Senator from Illinois.

    B. president of the United States.

    C. president of the Confederacy.

    D. commander of the Union army.

21. This man is known for writing the

    A. Dred Scott Decision.

    B. Missouri Compromise.

    C. Declaration of Independence.

    D. Emancipation Proclamation.

---

22. The period following the Civil War is called

    A. Constitution.

    B. Reconstruction.

    C. Manifest Destiny.

    D. Emancipation.

23. After the Civil War, Republicans in Congress believed that the South should be

    A. punished for starting the Civil War.

    B. permitted to make its own decisions.

    C. forced to restrict the rights of freed slaves.

    D. allowed to rebuild without interference.

24. What happened to African Americans in the South at the end of the period following the Civil War?

    A. They were kept in slavery.

    B. Each family was given 40 acres of land.

    C. They were given complete freedom and all rights.

    D. State laws were passed to keep them from being truly free.

UNIT
2

IN THIS UNIT

- Urban Industrial America

- America and the World

- World in Crisis

- World War to New Millennium

Left: *At the 1876 Centennial Exposition, only the hand and torch of the Statue of Liberty—not the whole statue—were on display. Organizers hoped to raise money to complete the statue, which was dedicated in 1886.*

U.S. History and Geography: 1877 to the Present

In the summer of 1876, Americans marked their 100th anniversary as an independent country. A great world's fair was held in Philadelphia. Nearly 10 million people visited in six months. They sampled strange new food items such as bananas and popcorn, and saw exhibits celebrating the scientific and cultural past and future of the United States.

As Americans looked back over their first century, they were excited by the fast growth of the new nation. They could not have imagined what was coming. Major changes in the cities were already under way. Within 25 years, their country would become a world power. Within 60 years, it would face its worst economic crisis. Within 100 years, it would have helped win two wars and lost another.

This unit is about the making of modern America.

Lesson 9

Urban Industrial America

IT'S IMPORTANT:

- Geography influenced the growth of American cities.

- Improved technology helped cities grow and cope with their growing pains.

- Waves of immigrants flocked to American cities between about 1880 and 1910.

- Political machines held power in many cities.

- The Progressive Movement set out to improve city life and government.

Following the Civil War and Reconstruction, Americans began moving to cities in great numbers. The reasons had to do with geography, technology, and opportunity. In 1876, the final year of Reconstruction, city dwellers made up 33 percent of the population. The 1920 census showed that more than half of Americans were living in urban areas that year. (In 1990, 75 percent of us lived in urban areas.)

Geography

Cities do not grow up by accident. There's always a reason for the growth of any urban place, large or small. Most of the major cities in the United States grew where they did because of geography. The five biggest American cities in 1820 were all ocean ports: New York, Philadelphia, Baltimore, Boston, and New Orleans. Ships gave these cities an easy link with the rest of the world.

Inland cities grew for two geographical reasons: closeness to raw materials and to a source of transportation. For example, Pittsburgh grew in the coal-mining region of western Pennsylvania where three major rivers came together. Minneapolis was centrally located in the grain belt where tons of wheat, corn, and other crops grew; and it was on the Mississippi River to boot.

Where railroad lines ran also was critical to whether cities would survive or die. History is filled with stories of towns that disappeared because a railroad line bypassed them in favor of a neighboring town. Omaha, Nebraska, is located on the Missouri River, but it grew into an important meat-packing center because of its railroad links. Cities such as Chicago, which combined railroads, water transportation capability, and industries of its own, became the most important cities in the country.

American cities became the centers of economic activity for hundreds of miles around. It was only natural that as their economic activity increased, their populations would, too.

Quick Review 1: Name some ways in which geography influenced the growth of cities.

_____

_____

_____

_____

Technology

American cities were home to factories that turned shipped-in raw materials to finished products that were shipped out across the United States and the world. The great change to industrial production began in the United States in the 1820s and was spreading throughout the northern states by 1850. The Civil War delayed industrialization in the southern states. By the time factories became widespread there, they also had come to the far west in California.

For the cities to attract workers, they had to be able to provide places for them to live and ways to get from place to place. Improved building technology made taller, stronger buildings possible. Cities experimented with systems for moving people from their homes to their jobs on commuter trains. After the invention of the automobile, street construction became a priority.

Cities also had to deal with problems brought about by thousands of people living close to one another. Fast-growing cities were often very dirty. A walk through the streets of an American city was often a smelly experience. Modern plumbing, sewage systems, and garbage collection were all in the future. Poor sanitation also led to disease. It was not uncommon for diseases such as **cholera** or **yellow fever** to sweep through a city, killing hundreds. Doctors didn't know how diseases were spread, and modern drugs were not available to fight them. When scientists discovered the link between poor sanitation and health, cities began planning ways to get clean water into neighborhoods and to get sewage and garbage out.

Even after cities began straightening out their sanitation problems, some problems remained. In the days before cars, horse-drawn carriages were used for transportation. As a result, streets were often covered with horse manure. People burned coal to heat homes and businesses, creating clouds of smoke. City life was noisy, too, day and night.

Quick Review 2: What were some problems facing cities as they grew?

_____

_____

_____

Opportunity

So why would people move to a crowded, dirty city? There was opportunity there. Farmers who had failed could find factory jobs. People from rural areas and small towns sometimes came seeking change or excitement. The cities were also magnets for people from other parts of the world.

During the first part of the 1800s, most immigrants to the United States came from northern and western Europe. They were headed for the farmlands of the Midwest and Great Plains. After 1880, however, a new wave of immigrants came to the United States. These people were from southern and eastern Europe, and they often ended up in eastern cities.

These waves of immigrants shared some things in common. They were looking for better opportunity than they could find on the small farms of their homelands. Some hoped to practice their religions with greater freedom than they were allowed at home. Some were fleeing war or oppression at home. The new immigrants often settled in communities with others from the same homeland and wrote letters back to Europe describing their experiences. Often, those left behind were eager to join their families and friends in America.

In 1892, the United States government set up an immigration center on **Ellis Island** in New York Harbor. Most of the second wave of immigrants passed through Ellis Island. After being checked in, immigrants were left to find their own way in American society. They often turned to their countrymen who were already here to find homes and jobs. Because immigrants often lived in communities with others who spoke their language and knew their customs, they were objects of suspicion. They sometimes faced discrimination in getting jobs at a fair rate of pay or finding decent housing.

Machines

During the years of greatest immigration (about 1880 to 1910), there was no such thing as unemployment insurance or welfare. If a person lost his or her job, or a family member died, there were few places to turn. In most city neighborhoods, however, there was at least one person who could help. He might find a job for a new immigrant or donate a turkey to a needy family at holiday time. In exchange, the immigrant owed only one thing: a vote for the right candidate on election day.

Powerful organizations called **political machines** often controlled city politics. The machines were organized from the top down, with representatives in almost every neighborhood of their cities. The machines were often corrupt. They bought votes and paid bribes to get and keep what they wanted. By doing favors for voters, they stayed in power. Machine politicians, known as **bosses**, often got rich. People knew about the corruption and bribery, yet it was accepted as a necessary price to keep city government running smoothly. To an immigrant family working long hours and trying to get by, such corruption didn't matter much. If a representative of the machine could offer help, they were willing to take it.

The Progressives

Sometimes, candidates would run for office promising to reform the system. They would not take bribes or pay them; they would do favors only if the favors were fair. While these candidates sometimes got elected, they rarely stayed in power for long.

As businesses grew in the 1880s and 1890s, the science of business management became important. People learned

Above: *Immigrant families often lived in crowded, dirty apartments called* **tenements**. *Although city inspectors sometimes checked the buildings, as the men in this photo are doing, there were few laws on tenement safety in many cities.*

How the Other Half Lives

Jacob Riis was an immigrant who became a journalist in New York. In 1890, his book, *How the Other Half Lives: Studies among the Tenements of New York*, shocked American readers with stories and pictures showing what immigrant life was like. Riis described the life of sales clerks in a department store:

"The investigation of the Working Women's Society disclosed the fact that wages averaged from $2 to $4.50 a week [and] were reduced by excessive fines . . . . A little girl, who received two dollars a week, made cash-sales amounting to $167 in a single day . . . yet for some trivial mistake the girl was fined 60 cents out of her two dollars. The practice prevailed in some stores of dividing the fines between the superintendent and the time-keeper at the end of the year. In one instance they amounted to $3,000, and 'the superintendent was heard to charge the time-keeper with not being strict enough in his duties.' One of the causes for fine in a certain large store was sitting down. The law requiring seats for saleswomen, generally ignored, was obeyed faithfully in this establishment. The seats were there, but the girls were fined when found using them."

that certain principles of management made businesses run more smoothly and earn more money. Some people began to wonder if the same principles that worked in business might work in government. These people were known as **Progressives**. The **Progressive Movement** was sparked by a sense that American life was getting worse, not better, for many Americans.

Factory workers often worked long hours in dangerous conditions for little pay. Children of immigrant families often had to work to help feed their families. Factory owners sometimes showed little concern for their workers. Although workers tried to form **unions**, their employers often fought them, sometimes violently. Unions were seen as a threat to the American ideal of hard work. Employers believed unions interfered with the right of an owner to run his or her business.

The conditions faced by immigrant workers and their families might have gone unnoticed if it hadn't been for the media. In the 1890s and early 1900s, a few major magazines such as *McClure's* and *Cosmopolitan* were being read all across the country. Magazine reporters uncovered criminal activity in government, unhealthy factory conditions, unsafe food production methods, and other scandals. These reporters, nicknamed **muckrakers**, played an important role in the Progressive Movement. When average Americans read about corruption, poverty, and disease in the cities, they often demanded that their leaders do something about it.

The Progressives tried to clean up corrupt city and state governments. Progressives battled political machines. They opened up the political process by favoring the secret ballot and primary elections. They called for regulation of public utilities such as electricity and water, to make sure consumers were not cheated. Progressives hoped to hold back the power of large corporations. They convinced state legislatures to set age limits for young workers and safety rules for all workers. They also argued that workers should have greater rights to form unions.

Quick Review 3: Why were muckrakers natural enemies of political machines?

_____

_____

_____

Progress

Progressive ideas remain a part of American life today. Franklin D. Roosevelt, whose New Deal policies shaped American government throughout the 20th century, was a Progressive as a young man. When voters decide a referendum question at the ballot box, they are using a Progressive idea. If your city has a city manager or city commission to run its government, that's Progressive, too.

Although the Progressive Movement cannot take all of the credit, American city life began to improve in the early 20th century. Better sanitation, safer homes and factories, and safer food and medicines helped raise life expectancies. Advances in medical care and nutrition, which began to develop in the early 1900s, also helped.

Life Expectancy at Birth

Race and gender	A person born in 1900 could expect to live to age:	A person born in 1995 could expect to live to age:
white male	48.2 years	73.4 years
all other races, male	32.5 years	67.9 years
white female	51.1 years	79.6 years
all other races, female	35.0 years	75.7 years

Source: *Information Please Almanac*

Left: *Today, vaccines exist for many childhood diseases, such as measles and whooping cough. In the days before such vaccines, childhood diseases were deadly. It was not uncommon for families to lose several children as infants. If a person born in 1900 lived through his or her first few years, his or her total life expectancy jumped by as much as 10 years.*

What Do You Think?

Directions: Answer the question on the lines provided. Be prepared to discuss your answer in class.

In a few American cities, political machines stayed in power until the 1970s. How could these machines keep running when most citizens knew how they operated?

_____

_____

_____

_____

Test Your Knowledge

Directions: Answer the questions on the lines provided.

1. How was access to transportation linked to the growth of cities?

   _____

   _____

   _____

   _____

2. Why did many employers resist the union movement?

   _____

   _____

   _____

   _____

3. Businesses became larger and more complex in the last years of the 1800s. How did this change help lead to the Progressive Movement?

   _____

   _____

   _____

   _____

By the 1890s, the Industrial Revolution had caused the economy of the United States to grow rapidly. American business and political leaders began to look to foreign countries as markets for goods produced in the United States. At the same time, European countries were expanding their own business activities in Asia and Africa. American leaders feared that the United States would be left behind. Some Americans also believed that the United States should set an example for the rest of the world as a land of democracy and freedom. In short, the United States was ready for its first steps onto the stage of world affairs.

Lesson 10

America and the World

Spanish-American War

Cuba, an island only 90 miles off the coast of Florida, fought for its independence from Spain in 1895. The revolt resulted in much bloodshed and serious damage to the Cuban economy, which included a great deal of American investment. Rediscovering the Monroe Doctrine, the United States insisted that the Spanish grant Cuba its independence and get out, but Spain refused. (You read about the Monroe Doctrine in Lesson 5.)

In early 1898, the U.S. Navy sent the warship *Maine* to Cuba to protect American citizens there. In February, the *Maine* exploded and sank in Havana harbor. Most Americans believed the Spanish were responsible. The United States declared war on Spain a few weeks later.

The **Spanish-American War** lasted throughout the summer of 1898. The most important battle was fought on the other side of the world, where the U.S. Navy captured the Philippine Islands, Spain's major colony in Asia. The most famous battle of the war occurred when U.S. soldiers, led by future president **Theodore Roosevelt**, captured San Juan Hill in Cuba. After Spain surrendered, it granted Cuba its independence. The United States bought the Philippines from Spain and received the island of Puerto Rico. The United States had become a player on the international stage.

IT'S IMPORTANT:

- The United States became an international power beginning with the Spanish-American War in 1898.

- President Theodore Roosevelt believed in big-stick diplomacy.

- The United States reluctantly entered World War I in 1917.

- Tariffs have been important to international trade throughout American history.

Quick Review 1: Give two reasons why the United States fought the Spanish-American War.

_____

_____

Roosevelt and the Monroe Doctrine

Theodore Roosevelt, who became president in 1901, believed in the Monroe Doctrine. Not only did it keep European countries from interfering in North and South America, but he felt it also gave the United States special rights as "policeman" in the region. American forces went to Cuba, Haiti, Nicaragua, Honduras, and the Dominican Republic to either support or remove governments, depending on what the United States felt its interests were. Roosevelt's view of America's role is often called *big-stick diplomacy*, from one of his favorite sayings: "Speak softly but carry a big stick." Roosevelt favored using American military power to protect the country's interests.

A famous example of big-stick diplomacy was the building of the **Panama Canal**. In 1903, Roosevelt helped Panama gain its independence from the South American nation of Colombia so that the United States could build the canal. The canal boosted American trade by cutting the sailing time of long ocean voyages. Before the canal, ships were forced to sail around the tip of South America. The Panama Canal allowed ships to cut through Central America instead.

World War I

American attention soon turned to events in Europe. **World War I** (known at the time as the Great War) broke out in 1914, with Great Britain, France, and several smaller countries on one side against Germany and its allies on the other.

The Monroe Doctrine said that the United States would not interfere in European affairs. At first, President **Woodrow Wilson** did his best to keep the United States out of the war, but its growing economic strength made that very difficult. American companies did millions of dollars in business with countries on both sides. In addition, Wilson believed that Great Britain and France were on the side of democracy and freedom.

It was only a matter of time before the United States would get involved in the war. When German submarines continued to attack American ships after being asked to stop, the United States declared war on April 6, 1917.

American soldiers helped the British and French to defeat Germany by November of 1918. President Wilson sailed to France for a peace conference. Wilson hoped that the conference would permit European nations big and small to determine their own futures. Wilson also proposed a new League of Nations that could head off future disputes before

Theodore Roosevelt

FAST FACT

The people of the Philippines believed their islands would become an independent country after the Spanish left. American leaders saw the islands as an important base for American trade in Asia. Therefore, the Philippines became a territory of the United States. Between 1899 and 1902, Filipino rebels fought unsuccessfully against American troops for independence.

they turned to war. He was frustrated on both counts. Instead of ensuring freedom and democracy for other countries, the victorious nations of Europe wanted to punish Germany. The United States Senate refused to allow the United States to join the League of Nations.

Quick Review 2: What two factors pushed the United States into World War I?

_____

_____

_____

_____

> ❝ *What we demand in this war. . . .is that the world be made fit and safe to live in; and particularly that it be made safe for every peace-loving nation which, like our own, wishes to live its own life, determine its own institutions, [and] be assured of justice and fair dealing by the other peoples of this world [instead of] force and selfish aggression.* ❞
>
> —Woodrow Wilson, 1918

Neutrality and War

When the Senate refused to allow the United States to participate in the League of Nations, its action reflected the American public's mood. During the 1920s, the United States tried to stay out of world affairs, except for trade. Even in the 1930s, when it began to look as if Germany would again plunge Europe into war, the United States remained **isolationist**. After World War II began in 1939, the United States tried to maintain official **neutrality**. Economic ties and a preference for democracy instead of dictatorship soon tilted the United States toward the British and French side against the Germans. You'll read more about World War II in Lessons 11 and 12.

Tariffs and Trade

A **tariff** is a tax placed on goods that one country imports from another. At one time, tariffs were a major source of money for governments. Thanks to modern tax policies,

FAST FACT

American soldiers did not begin fighting in Europe until early in 1918. More than 116,000 died of wounds and disease in about 10 months. The numbers include thousands who died of the flu when a great epidemic swept the world in the late summer and fall of 1918.

Up Close:

Great Britain and Germany

In 1900, if you had asked an average American whether the United States would fight on the same side with Great Britain or Germany in a war, that American probably would have said "Germany." The United States was home to many German immigrants, while Britain had been a frequent enemy. The United States fought Britain in the Revolutionary War, fought them again during the War of 1812, and nearly went to war with them in 1895 over a border dispute in South America.

Above: *American soldiers didn't begin fighting in Europe until 1918. These combat engineers are returning from the battle of St. Mihiel in eastern France.*

The relationship changed after the 1895 dispute was settled. Britain realized that Germany was becoming a threat to peace in Europe. They decided that friendship with the United States might be useful in the event of war. Britain also had become more democratic during the 1800s. In fact, the British now believed in some of the same ideals that had caused the American colonists to declare their independence. The history shared by the two countries contributed to their growing closeness as well. So, in World War I, the United States and Britain found themselves on the same side.

The war brought suspicion onto German Americans. People feared that anyone with a German last name might be a spy. Some communities made it illegal to speak German or teach it in schools. At least one American city named "Germantown" changed its name to "Liberty." Sauerkraut, a popular German dish, was renamed "liberty cabbage."

As the war went on, it became dangerous for anyone, German or not, to speak against the American government. New laws made it illegal to say anything that might harm the war effort. Although the Constitution still included the right of free speech, people trying to use it occasionally ended up in jail.

governments no longer depend on tariffs for money. Instead, tariffs are used most often to protect industries from foreign competition. Here's an example: If a French company must pay a high tariff on products it wants to sell in the United States, it will have to charge a higher price to consumers for those products. The same products made by American companies will cost less. Historically, tariffs have been good for American producers and bad for those who want or need to buy foreign products.

Tariffs were high during most of the 1800s. As the volume of world trade began to grow in the early 1900s, some American leaders argued that tariffs ought to be cut. If the United States cut its tariffs, other countries might do the same. The result would be more trade dollars flowing through American businesses.

Tariffs were raised and lowered several times between 1909 and 1930. Republican presidents tended to favor high tariffs while Democrats preferred lower tariffs. The best-known American tariff was the **Smoot-Hawley Tariff Act** of 1930, which was named for the two members of Congress who wrote it. The Smoot-Hawley Tariff Act raised tariffs to their highest levels in 100 years. It was supposed to help American industries deal with the terrible economic conditions of the Great Depression. Instead, it made things worse. The total volume of world trade dropped sharply.

Since the Depression, most countries around the world have encouraged **free trade**, with few or no tariffs. Tariffs still exist today, though; the United States government often uses them to punish countries that trade unfairly.

What Do You Think?

Directions: Answer the question on the lines provided. Be prepared to discuss your answers in class.

Imagine that you are President Wilson in 1916. You are willing to help the countries at war in Europe to negotiate what you call "peace without victory," but you are not willing to send troops to fight. Can you uphold freedom and democracy in this way? Give reasons for your answer.

_____

_____

_____

_____

_____

Test Your Knowledge

Directions: Fill in the blank in each sentence.

1. Spain's refusal to leave the island of Cuba led to the _____ in the summer of 1898.

2. President _____ believed in big-stick diplomacy.

3. The United States used its big stick to get the land for building the

   _____ in Central America.

4. From 1914 to 1917, President _____ tried to keep the United States out

   of _____.

5. The _____ was an international organization designed to keep disagreements between countries from turning to war.

6. During the 1920s and 1930s, American foreign policy was _____.

7. The _____ Tariff Act of 1930 is blamed by some people for making the Great Depression worse than it already was.

Directions: Answer the questions on the lines provided.

8. Why did the United States become more involved in foreign affairs at the end of the 1800s?

   _____

   _____

   _____

   _____

   _____

   _____

9. Why couldn't the United States stay out of World War I?

_____

_____

_____

_____

_____

_____

_____

Lesson 11

World in Crisis

World War I was the world's first industrialized war. No war in history had been so successful at killing people in large numbers. Woodrow Wilson once called it "the war to end all wars." Wilson and others hoped that humankind would find a way to settle differences without war, especially since modern weapons had made war so terrible. Yet only 20 years later, the world exploded into an even more destructive war.

Europe Between the Wars

After World War I, Europe was an unstable place. Millions of people had died. Cities and farms had been destroyed. Everywhere, the old ways of life were gone.

Even before the war ended, Russia went through historic change. In 1917, revolutionaries overthrew the **tsar** (king). After months of instability, a group called the **Bolsheviks** took control of the government. They were lead by Vladimir **Lenin**, who followed Karl Marx's idea that workers should overthrow industrial capitalism and create a communist society. Civil war between the Bolsheviks and their enemies lasted until 1921. In 1922, the Bolsheviks organized the Union of Soviet Socialist Republics, also known as the **Soviet Union**.

After the death of Lenin in 1924, **Joseph Stalin** took power in the Soviet Union. He was less interested in establishing a communist society than he was in building a powerful industrial economy under his dictatorial control. Stalin killed his enemies by the thousands. He forced small farmers to give up their lands to large, government-run collective farms. Those who resisted were imprisoned or killed. When farm production fell, as many as 10 million Soviet citizens died of starvation. Stalin would rule until his death in 1953.

In Germany after World War I, the government was unable to keep the economy from falling apart. Many Germans believed their leaders had betrayed them by signing an unfair treaty to end the war. Italy also had problems. Its economy was weak, and its government was ineffective. Citizens of both countries began looking for solutions to their problems.

Italians found a solution in the **Fascist** party (pronounced *FASH-ist*), led by **Benito Mussolini**. Fascists set out to unite all parts of Italian society under one ruler. The government would control business, but it also would protect private property and private enterprise. To strengthen the country, Mussolini made all other political parties illegal and gave himself a great deal of power to make laws.

In Germany, many groups competed for power. Communists argued that they had the answer. German fascists claimed that Germany needed powerful leadership and not democracy. When the German economy collapsed in the 1920s, Germans became even more desperate to find a way out.

Some Germans found it in the **Nazi** party, led by **Adolf Hitler**. Hitler told many of them what they wanted to hear: that they hadn't really lost World War I and that the biggest problem they faced was a government that couldn't help them. But Hitler added something else to his political program. He was violently anti-Semitic. He blamed Jews for many of Germany's problems. Hitler claimed that the German people belonged to a superior race, **Aryans**, who were the rightful rulers of the world.

Both Hitler and Mussolini were extreme **nationalists**. They encouraged strong patriotism among their followers. They argued that service to the Italian or German state was the greatest duty of every citizen. They also were strongly anti-communist. As the economic crisis of the Great Depression swept over the world, both the Fascists and Nazis gained followers. By 1932, the Nazi party was the strongest in Germany. Hitler became chancellor (leader of the government) in 1933 and quickly moved to increase his power. Within a year, Hitler was the absolute ruler of Germany.

Quick Review 1: Why was Hitler viewed as a threat by many Europeans outside Germany?

_____

_____

_____

Prohibition

As you read in Lesson 10, Americans wanted to stay out of the world's business after World War I. They found plenty of ways to keep their minds off of world affairs. The decade of the 1920s was one of the most eventful in American history.

For nearly 100 years, some Americans had argued that alcohol was the cause of many of society's problems. They blamed drunkenness for causing poverty and crime, and claimed that a sensible way to fight both problems was to ban alcohol. The **temperance movement** gained strength state by state. By 1917, the sale and consumption of alcohol was illegal in nearly half of the states. In 1919, the **Eighteenth Amendment** was added to the Constitution. It banned alcohol everywhere in the United States. **Prohibition** had begun.

The trouble with Prohibition was that it was very difficult to enforce. **Moonshiners** made their own liquor; **bootleggers** sold the homemade liquor or smuggled liquor into the United States from other countries. Criminal organizations soon learned that the illegal liquor trade was very profitable. Many public officials took bribes to leave the bootlegging businesses alone. Wars broke out between rival organizations.

Americans did not lose their taste for liquor overnight. **Speakeasies**, illegal nightclubs that sold liquor, were easy to find in most places. In short, anyone who wanted an alcoholic drink during the 1920s could get one. In 1933, the great temperance experiment ended with the **Twenty-First Amendment** to the Constitution, which repealed the Eighteenth. National Prohibition was over, although alcohol remains illegal in some parts of the United States to this day.

The Suffrage Movement

Although the Founding Fathers talked a lot about liberty, freedom, and rights, a large number of Americans were left out. Women had few legal rights until the middle of the 1800s. In many states, a woman could not own property. Anything she had became the legal property of her husband, and if her husband died, the property passed immediately to a male child. Women often could not make contracts, and although their husbands could divorce them, it was much harder for them to divorce their husbands.

In 1848, the Seneca Falls Convention was the first major meeting of the women's rights movement. One of the convention's goals was to change unfair laws. These efforts found success beginning in the 1850s, but it took much longer to win the right to vote. Women's rights leaders of the 19th century, such as Lucretia Mott, Elizabeth Cady Stanton, and Susan B. Anthony, argued that equal rights were a matter of simple logic. On July 4, 1876, Anthony told a crowd: "We ask of our rulers . . . no special privileges, no special legislation. We ask justice, we ask equality, we ask that all civil and political rights that belong to citizens of the United States be guaranteed to us and our daughters forever."

Many Americans of both genders fought against women's **suffrage** (the right to vote). Some shared the opinion of former president Grover Cleveland: "Sensible and responsible women do not want to vote. The relative positions to be assumed by men and women in the working out of our civilization were assigned long ago by a higher intelligence than ours." Yet as new western states joined the Union, their state constitutions gave women the right to vote in state elections. After more than 70 years of struggle, the **Nineteenth Amendment** was ratified in 1920, giving women the right to vote in all elections.

Women's Suffrage, 1919

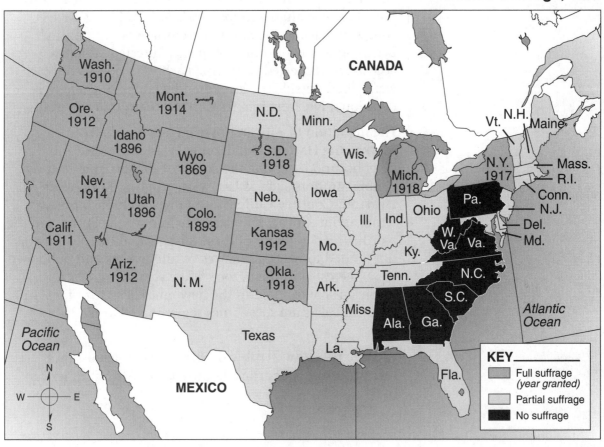

Some Americans thought that voting patterns might change once women were involved. As years went by, this didn't happen. What happened instead was that women began moving into positions in government. Frances Perkins became the first female cabinet member (secretary of labor) in 1933. Nevertheless, the women's rights movement did not go out of business. As early as 1923, at a 75th anniversary celebration of the Seneca Falls Convention, delegates proposed that an Equal Rights Amendment should be added to the Constitution to go beyond the Nineteenth Amendment. American women are still waiting for that.

African American Life and Culture

While women were gaining new rights, African Americans were fighting a losing battle against segregation. In most of the South, state laws required separate public facilities for whites and blacks. Voting laws were written so that it was nearly impossible for blacks to vote. As a result, millions of African Americans headed north. They left the rural South for northern and western cities, such as New York, Chicago, Detroit, and Los Angeles.

Although there were fewer laws restricting them outside the South, African Americans still faced prejudice in the North. Riots between angry groups of whites and blacks were common. Back in the South, **lynching** was not unusual. Lynching was a form of mob justice directed at blacks accused or suspected of crimes. Each year, dozens of blacks were killed outside the law, often by hanging. There were occasional lynching incidents in Northern states as well.

The migration of African Americans to Northern cities sparked the **Harlem Renaissance**. Harlem, a New York neighborhood, became the center of African American culture. Authors such as **Langston Hughes**, **Zora Neale Hurston**, **Countee Cullen**, and **James Weldon Johnson** wrote about African American life in both the South and the North. The popularity of these authors and their works was not limited to black audiences. White readers and publishers were interested in them, too. At the same time, black musicians contributed to the new musical style of **jazz**. In fact, the 1920s are sometimes remembered as the Jazz Age.

Quick Review 2: How did the Harlem Renaissance increase white Americans' knowledge of African American life?

_____

_____

_____

Entertainment

Americans of the 1920s and 1930s could do more for fun than just read and listen to jazz. Radio and movies were popular new media. Movies were silent until the late 1920s. Viewers watched the screen as a piano or organ played music to set the scenes. Although words sometimes appeared on the screen, silent movie actors did most of their acting with gestures and facial expressions. The first movie with sound,

The Jazz Singer, was released in 1927. By the 1930s, Americans were spending millions of dollars on movie tickets. Theaters sometimes got new films as often as twice a week.

Radio started off as a hobby for gadget-makers in the early 1920s. By 1930, 40 percent of American homes had a radio. (Even during the economic crisis of the Great Depression, sales of radios stayed strong.) Most radio entertainment was performed live, even on small local stations. Recording tape did not exist. Many radio stations frowned upon playing recorded music. Like television today, radio had comedies, cop shows, soap operas, and sports broadcasts.

Radio also became a major news source. In 1927, when American **Charles Lindbergh** became the first pilot to fly nonstop by himself across the Atlantic, radio flashed the news to listeners around the country. In the 1930s, President Franklin Roosevelt made radio speeches about his programs. These informal talks were known as **fireside chats** because people could sit in their living rooms near the fireplace and listen. As Europe began to slide toward war in the late 1930s, Americans followed the news on radio. In addition, national radio networks brought big-name entertainers into American homes. Comedian **Jack Benny**, humorous news commentator **Will Rogers**, and dozens of others became well known across the country by performing on radio.

Driving for pleasure became a popular way of spending time in the 1920s. Like most new consumer technology, cars were a luxury item and status symbol at first, but not for long. **Henry Ford** began producing his famous **Model T** in 1909. By use of the assembly line, the **Ford Motor Company** could produce cars in large numbers, which lowered the price. By 1925, a Model T cost just $290. By 1930, there were 23 million registered cars on the road.

The automobile made Americans more mobile. Industries supplying parts and materials to carmakers grew prosperous. Cars sparked the growth of paved roads and suburbs, both of which boosted the construction industry. The automobile helped build the tourism industry, as Americans were free to travel more easily.

The Great Depression

Another name for the Jazz Age was the **Roaring '20s**. The American economy was certainly roaring during the 1920s. Factories were more productive than they had ever been. Government policies were very friendly to business growth. Corporations and their investors made money, which they poured into the stock market. Average Americans were eager to invest also. Stock prices rose so fast that people poured their life savings into the market, sure that they could cash in.

Advertisers encouraged Americans to buy products on credit. People bought radios, washing machines, and vacuum cleaners and promised to pay for them later. As a result, personal debt rose at a faster rate than personal income.

Although it seemed to some people like everyone was getting rich, there was a growing gap between the richest and poorest Americans. Tariff laws slowed international trade. American farmers couldn't produce enough to pay their debts. Many banks were poorly managed and unsafe. These factors and others made the economy much weaker than it seemed.

Market experts predicted that the good times couldn't last forever. In October 1929, the good times ended. Stocks lost $5 billion in value in one afternoon. Investors began selling their stock, hoping to get something before it became worthless, which only drove prices lower. Billions more in losses followed over the next few days. The **stock market crash** cost investors billions and triggered the **Great Depression**. America's financial troubles soon spread around the world.

Businesses failed. Workers lost their jobs and were unable to pay for food or medical care. Some lost their homes and farms. President **Herbert Hoover** believed that it wasn't the government's job to heal the economy or help citizens. He believed that the American economy would pull itself out of the Depression if it were left alone. He preferred that private groups help needy Americans.

Hoover quickly became the most unpopular man in America. The Republican Party renominated him for president in 1932, but the Democrats knew that almost any candidate would have a good chance at beating Hoover. The Democrats nominated **Franklin D. Roosevelt**, governor of New York. Unlike Hoover, Roosevelt promised to attack the Depression. Roosevelt won by a landslide.

" I pledge you, I pledge myself, to a new deal for the American people. "

—Franklin D. Roosevelt, 1932

Quick Review 3: What were some factors contributing to the Great Depression?

_____

_____

_____

_____

The New Deal

Franklin Roosevelt, also known as **FDR**, believed that Americans needed three types of programs to escape the Depression: relief programs for needy people, recovery programs to boost economic growth, and reform programs to make sure such a crisis would never happen again. Roosevelt's programs were nicknamed the **New Deal**, after his campaign slogan. Within the first 100 days after he took office in March 1933, Roosevelt created a series of agencies that funneled government money to citizens in exchange for useful work. Other agencies had the job of giving aid to people who needed it.

Some New Deal Agencies

Agency	Purpose
Civilian Conservation Corps (CCC)	Improved forests, rivers, and other natural resource areas through conservation projects
Civil Works Administration (CWA)	Built roads, parks, schools, airports; cleaned up and rebuilt rundown neighborhoods
Public Works Administration (PWA)	Built large-scale engineering projects such as bridges, power plants, and dams
Home Owners Loan Corporation (HOLC)	Helped homeowners refinance mortgages
Agriculture Adjustment Administration (AAA)	Helped control farm production to boost prices for cattle and crops

FDR also hoped to set up a government agency to set prices and minimum wage levels. The **National Recovery Administration** (NRA) would limit competition and keep more businesses operating. The Supreme Court later declared the NRA unconstitutional.

One of the most famous New Deal agencies was the **Works Progress Administration (WPA)**. The WPA gave people jobs building roads, playgrounds, swimming pools, sidewalks, and sewers right in their hometowns. In addition, the WPA hired artists and writers for local history and public art projects. The **National Youth Administration**, part of WPA, put people between ages 16 and 25 to work at after-school jobs around their high schools and colleges. NYA members mowed lawns, painted walls, and did other jobs. Between 1935 and the end of the WPA in 1943, one out of every four Americans had held a WPA job.

The New Deal also gave Americans the **Social Security** system. Employees and employers pay into a Social Security fund. Then, when a worker reaches retirement age, he or she can collect a monthly check. Social Security also pays benefits to disabled workers and the spouses and children of workers who died before they reached retirement age.

The New Deal transformed American government. It became more active in shaping society and helping citizens directly than ever before. Roosevelt strengthened the office of the president, taking a stronger leadership role in directing public policy than most previous presidents. He was the first president to assume what we think of as the current role of the president, as the central figure in the American government.

Quick Review 4: How did the New Deal mark a major change in the role of American government?

_____

_____

_____

_____

World War—Again

While Americans were struggling against the Great Depression, Adolf Hitler was building what he called the **Third Reich** (rhymes with *hike*). He imagined a great empire in Europe that would last for a thousand years. He built up the German army and planned to increase the size of German territory. Because Hitler believed that the peoples of eastern Europe were not members of the Aryan race, he also believed he had the right to take their lands and rule them.

In March 1938, Hitler made a deal with Germany's neighbor, Austria, to unite the two countries. Although this union was a violation of the treaty that ended World War I, other European countries did not resist it. Few Europeans had a great desire to fight another war so soon after the last one. British prime minister **Neville Chamberlain** believed it was better to give Hitler what he wanted now and hope to make a deal with him later. Historians call his policy **appeasement**.

In September 1938, Hitler made a move to take over part of Czechoslovakia called the **Sudetenland**. At a conference in

Alphabet Soup

In addition to the Social Security Administration, other New Deal agencies are still operating today. Like other New Deal agencies, most are known as well by their initials as by their names. The Federal Deposit Insurance Corporation (FDIC) insures bank deposits; the Securities and Exchange Commission (SEC) regulates the stock market; the National Labor Relations Board (NLRB) protects and regulates labor unions; the Federal Housing Administration (FHA) offers loans and insurance to homeowners.

Up Close:

TVA

The valley of the Tennessee River covers more than 40 thousand square miles. It includes most of Tennessee and parts of Kentucky, Virginia, North Carolina, Georgia, Alabama, and Mississippi. When the valley was first settled, farmers and miners took down trees, planted crops, and mined the land. But the cycle of floods from the valley rivers, soil erosion, and deforestation caused problems for the region. It was one of the poorest areas of the United States. Rural communities were primitive, with no electricity.

Above: *Norris Dam in Tennessee*

As part of the New Deal, the U.S. government set up the **Tennessee Valley Authority** (TVA). TVA's purpose was to control flooding, improve river transportation, and produce cheap electricity through a series of dams and fuel-powered plants. By doing all this, TVA would also improve the region's economy.

The TVA is still operating today, and has been a great success in achieving its goals. More than 50 dams now control spring flooding. Some of the land has been planted with new trees. The remaining land has regained its agricultural and mining productivity. The rivers can better handle products by the cheapest form of transportation possible—barge traffic. The region's dams, 12 coal-fired generating plants, and two nuclear power plants, can produce up to 30 million kilowatts of electric power. Businesses and homes in the Tennessee Valley have some of the cheapest electric bills in the nation.

Conservation and recreation are also part of the TVA's mission. The government requires coal companies who have strip-mined the land to restore it. The many lakes and reservoirs of the Tennessee Valley provide great recreational opportunities for Valley residents. In addition, the TVA sends some of its profits back to the federal government, so taxpayers everywhere see some benefits.

Before TVA, the Tennessee Valley was poverty-stricken and backward. The area now has a thriving economy with diverse industries and a beautiful landscape. The TVA has helped bring vitality to the Tennessee Valley.

The First Lady

Today, Americans expect the wife of the president to be involved in public issues of some kind. It wasn't always this way. The first First Lady to become famous in her own right was **Eleanor Roosevelt.**

Eleanor Roosevelt married Franklin, her distant cousin, in 1905. In 1921, Franklin contracted polio. The disease made him unable to walk without heavy braces on his legs. He used a wheelchair most of the time. Afterward, Eleanor began making political trips and working as her husband's eyes and ears. After FDR was elected president in 1932, she wrote a daily newspaper column and magazine articles and hosted a radio show. She was an adviser to the president behind the scenes, pushing him to help minorities and the poor. Following her husband's death in 1945, she became a delegate to the United Nations, where she was chair of the Human Rights Commission and helped write the UN's Universal Declaration of Human Rights. She remained active in Democratic party politics almost up until she died in 1962.

Munich, Germany, Britain, France, and Italy agreed to permit Hitler to take over the Sudetenland if he promised not to take the rest of Czechoslovakia. Hitler agreed. Six months later, Hitler went back on his agreement and took the rest of Czechoslovakia.

Chamberlain's policy of appeasement was clearly a failure. When Hitler began looking toward Poland, Britain announced that it would defend Poland against a German invasion. On September 1, 1939, the German army crossed the Polish border. Two days later, Britain and France declared war. For the second time in 25 years, Europe was at war. (Not long after, Neville Chamberlain was out as British prime minister.)

Americans and War

Americans followed the Munich crisis closely. (It was one of the first major news stories ever covered on radio.) Yet Americans were still in no mood to get involved. Congress passed a series of **Neutrality Acts** forbidding the United States to sell weapons or give help to countries at war. Even when France was taken over and Britain threatened, many Americans claimed we should stay out of the war.

President Roosevelt was not one of those Americans. Roosevelt and British Prime Minister **Winston Churchill** had a close relationship. In 1940, the two leaders made an agreement, the **Lend-Lease Act**, which gave American ships and supplies to Britain and the Soviet Union. Roosevelt had promised "all measures short of war" to help. As it turned out, war was coming to the United States, but not from a direction most people expected.

Throughout the 1930s, Japan had moved to increase its power in Asia. It fought a war with China starting in 1937. When war began in Europe, the Japanese supported Germany and took over French and Dutch territories in Asia.

The United States cut off sales of oil and scrap metal to the Japanese. The two countries tried to make a deal. All the while they were talking, however, the Japanese were planning a surprise attack. It came on **December 7, 1941**, at the American naval base at **Pearl Harbor**, Hawaii. The attack killed 2,500 Americans, sank or damaged eight battleships, destroyed 188 airplanes, and shocked the American people. The next day, Roosevelt asked Congress to declare war on Japan. Germany and Italy immediately declared war on the United States. The country that had tried to stay out of world affairs since 1918 would now fight two wars on opposite sides of the world.

> *Yesterday, December 7, 1941—a date which will live in infamy—the United States of America was suddenly and deliberately attacked by naval and air forces of the empire of Japan. . . . No matter how long it may take us to overcome this premeditated invasion, the American people in their righteous might will win through to absolute victory.*
>
> —**Franklin D. Roosevelt**, speaking to Congress on December 8, 1941

Quick Review 5: How did the United States get into two wars at the same time in 1941?

_____

_____

_____

_____

Concentration Camps in America

The West Coast of the United States was home to thousands of Japanese Americans. Some were American citizens who had been born here. There was a fear that some might be disloyal to the United States, however. In 1942, more than 100,000 Japanese Americans were moved from their homes to special relocation camps inland until the war ended. Although these camps were not as horrible as German concentration camps in Europe, what they stood for was bad enough. The American Civil Liberties Union called the internment of Japanese Americans "the worst single wholesale violation of civil liberties of American citizens in our history." In 1988, Congress ordered that Japanese Americans who had been held in the camps should receive compensation from the federal government.

What Do You Think?

Directions: Answer the questions on the lines provided. Be prepared to discuss your answers in class.

1. Do the lessons Americans learned during Prohibition have any value in today's fight against tobacco and illegal drug use? Give reasons for your answer.

   _____

   _____

   _____

   _____

   _____

   _____

2. How does the New Deal continue to affect the lives of Americans today?

   _____

   _____

   _____

   _____

   _____

   _____

Test Your Knowledge

Directions: In each group of four, one item does not belong with the other three. Circle the one that does not belong, then explain why it does not belong on the lines provided.

1. bootleggers
   temperance
   suffrage
   speakeasies

   _____

   _____

   _____

2. Frances Perkins
   Lucretia Mott
   Susan B. Anthony
   Elizabeth Cady Stanton

   _____

   _____

   _____

3. Zora Neale Hurston
   Charles Lindbergh
   James Weldon Johnson
   Langston Hughes

   _____

   _____

   _____

4. stock market crash
   poorly managed banks
   gap between rich and poor
   attack on Pearl Harbor

   _____

   _____

   _____

5. UN
   TVA
   WPA
   FDIC

   _____

   _____

   _____

Directions: Answer the question on the lines below.

6. What was appeasement?

   _____

   _____

   _____

   _____

   _____

   _____

   _____

   _____

In early 1942, it looked as if the United States and its allies might lose what soon became known as World War II. The Germans had won a string of victories in Europe and North Africa going back to 1939. The Japanese took over more and more of the Pacific Ocean region. Franklin Roosevelt's pledge of "absolute victory" seemed shaky.

In 1942, however, the United States was still gearing up its war effort. Factories of every kind were changing over to war production. For example, auto plants started making planes and tanks. Many consumer goods were **rationed** at home, so that troops in the war zones would have the supplies they needed to fight. Men joined the army and navy, leaving women to do important war work at home. In some American factories, the workforce was up to 90 percent female. **Rosie the Riveter** was a symbol of the American woman in the workforce.

By late 1942, the United States was a full partner in the war effort—and the results began to show. Planes and tanks rolled off the assembly lines and onto the battlefields, where Allied armies began to win.

Before the war, Germany and the Soviet Union had signed a **non-aggression pact**. Although Germany had agreed not to attack the Soviet Union, Adolf Hitler broke his word again. The June 1941 decision to attack the Soviet Union may have cost Germany the war. Hitler sent millions of men and tons of weapons and other supplies to the eastern front, but the Soviet army held on. In 1943 and 1944, Soviet troops began pushing the Germans back.

The Soviet effort against the Germans had a terrible price. More than seven million Soviet soldiers died in the war, along with 15 million civilians, far greater casualty figures than any other country.

Endings

In the spring of 1945, the war news was mostly good, except, of course, for the families who learned their husbands or fathers had died in battle somewhere in Europe or the Pacific. But on the afternoon of April 12, most Americans began feeling as though there had been a death in the family. President Roosevelt died suddenly. He had been in office since 1933. He was the only president many Americans had ever known. He had done much to pull the United States out of the Great Depression and lead it to victory in World War II. Yet it would be up to the new president, **Harry Truman**, to finish the job Roosevelt and the country had started.

World War to New Millennium

IT'S IMPORTANT:

- World War II had a terrible cost.

- The Cold War between the U.S. and the Soviet Union lasted for nearly 50 years.

- Korea, Cuba, and Vietnam were Cold War contests.

- At the end of the Cold War in 1992, the United States became the world's only superpower.

- African Americans and women worked for equal rights.

- The Watergate scandal was an important event of the 1970s.

WORLD WAR II TIMELINE

1941

December 7:
Japanese attack Pearl Harbor, Hawaii

1942

June:
United States defeats Japan at the Battle of Midway

1942

August 7:
First major Allied offensive in the Pacific begins at Guadalcanal Island

1942

November 8:
Allied army invades northern Africa

1943

July 10:
Allied army invades Italy

1944

June 6:
D-Day–Allied army invades France

1944

October:
U.S. Navy destroys Japanese Naval forces at Leyte Gulf

As the Soviet Red Army pushed across Europe from the east, Allied troops were heading toward Germany from the west. In April 1945, Americans and Soviets met along the Elbe River in Germany. Hitler knew the end was near, and on April 30, he committed suicide. One week later, Germany surrendered.

In the Pacific, the slow process of pushing back the Japanese was looking successful. The goal was to take back what the Japanese had captured, one island at a time if necessary. Each island would be a stepping-stone to taking the next one. The campaign took nearly three years. When American troops captured **Iwo Jima** and **Okinawa** in the spring and summer of 1945, the end seemed near. Yet the Japanese had fought so fiercely that American military planners feared a million Allied soldiers might be killed or wounded in an invasion of Japan.

Before taking office, Truman had never heard of the **Manhattan Project**. This top-secret effort involved scientists from around the world in building the most powerful weapon the world had ever seen: the atomic bomb. The United States wanted to build it before the Germans did. In July 1945, the bomb was successfully tested. It contained the destructive power of thousands of tons of dynamite, generated tremendous heat, and released deadly radiation.

Three weeks later, Truman ordered the bomb to be dropped on Japan. The cities of **Hiroshima** and **Nagasaki** were bombed on August 6 and 9, 1945. It is unclear exactly how many people died in the bombings or from the effects of radiation afterward. The number is most likely in the hundreds of thousands. The Japanese surrendered a few days after the Nagasaki bombing.

Was the A-Bomb Necessary?

Historians are still debating whether the nuclear attacks on Japan were necessary. Some argue that Japan would have collapsed after a few more weeks of fighting. They say the estimate of one million casualties in an Allied invasion was far too high. Some historians think Truman may have dropped the bomb to send a message to the Soviet Union about Allied power. Even though the Soviets were on the Allied side in World War II, they were a communist country. It seemed clear that they could easily become an enemy once the war ended. As you will read later in this lesson, that's exactly what happened.

The Cost

There's no way to know exactly how many people died in World War II. Estimates say that 13 million soldiers died and more than 23 million were wounded. Worldwide, as many as 75 million people may have died. Millions more lost their homes and possessions.

During the war, there were a few stories that the Germans were running an organized campaign to kill European Jews. In 1945, Allied troops discovered concentration camps in Poland and Germany. Hitler's anti-Semitism was well known, yet the depth of it came as a shock. The purpose of the camps was simple: they existed as places where Jews would be shipped and killed. Estimates say that six million Jewish men, women, and children died in places such as **Auschwitz** and **Dachau**. Six million others probably died in the camps, too: members of other "non-Aryan" races, political prisoners, and disabled people. The mass killing is remembered as the **Holocaust**. Ever since, Jews have kept a simple motto in mind: "Never again." They have vowed to never let the world forget what happened in the camps.

The Allies rounded up the leaders of Germany and Japan and put them on trial. In 1947, 17 Nazi leaders were convicted of crimes against humanity at **Nuremberg**, Germany. Ten of them were sentenced to death. Also executed was the Japanese general **Hideki Tojo**, who had ordered the attack on Pearl Harbor.

The war redrew the map of Europe for the second time in 30 years. It gave birth to a new international organization, the **United Nations**, to replace the League of Nations, which had failed to stop the war from coming. The war left the United States as the world's most powerful nation. And it changed the lives of every American, even those who would not be born until after it was over.

WORLD WAR II TIMELINE

1944

December:
Battle of the Bulge begins; Germans make strong stand before defeat in January 1945

1945

April 12:
Franklin Roosevelt dies; Harry Truman becomes president

1945

May 8:
VE Day–Germany surrenders; war ends in Europe

1945

August 6 and 9:
United States drops atomic bombs on Hiroshima and Nagasaki

1945

September 2:
Japan surrenders; World War II ends

Quick Review 1: What was the Holocaust?

_____

_____

_____

_____

_____

Cold War

Even before World War II was over, the world was taking sides once again. Although the Soviet Union fought on the Allied side, it refused to remove its armies from Eastern Europe after the war. The war-weary nations of Western Europe distrusted the Soviets, but they were too weak to defend themselves. As a result, the United States took responsibility for defending the West.

This tense face-off, known as the **Cold War**, lasted for nearly 50 years. The war was unusual in the sense that no Soviet army ever fired a shot at an American army. Yet like other American wars in the 20th century, it was a contest between democracy and dictatorship. The Soviet Union hoped to increase its strength by converting other governments to **communism**, a dictatorial political and economic system that denied freedom and opportunity to its citizens. Meanwhile, the United States committed itself to **containment**—stopping the spread of communism and promoting the growth of democracy around the world.

One way the United States hoped to promote democracy was by helping the damaged economies of Europe to rebuild. The **Marshall Plan**, proposed by Secretary of State George Marshall in 1947, gave billions of dollars to European countries to repair factories and mines. Countries receiving money were required to spend some of it with American companies, so the Marshall Plan also provided a boost to the American economy.

The Cold War soon spread from Europe to Asia. When **China** came under Communist control in 1949, many Americans began talking of an international Communist conspiracy, pitting the combined muscle of China and the Soviets against the United States. In such an atmosphere, almost any conflict anywhere in the world threatened to turn the Cold War into a hot one.

As long as the United States was the only country in the world with nuclear weapons, it held the upper hand. Once the Soviet Union developed its own atomic bomb, in 1949, the balance of power changed. The two **superpowers** began building large numbers of more powerful weapons. The nuclear **arms race** meant growing danger. A possible nuclear war, with millions of civilians dying on both sides in a matter of minutes, was almost too terrible to think about, yet the possibility seemed very real.

At the present moment in world history nearly every nation must choose between alternative ways of life. The choice is too often not a free one.

—**Harry Truman,** 1947

Quick Review 2: What was the basic conflict in the Cold War?

_____

_____

_____

Korea and McCarthy

After World War I, the victorious nations formed the League of Nations, a worldwide organization designed to prevent future conflicts before they turned to war. Because the U.S. Senate would not approve the treaty ending the war, the United States never joined the League. After World War II, the United States helped to organize a new international organization, the **United Nations** (UN). The usefulness of the UN would be tested almost immediately.

In the summer of 1950, North Korean troops invaded South Korea. Immediately, the United Nations jumped to the defense of South Korea. China aided the North. Many people believed the **Korean War** would turn into World War III, the first (and last) nuclear war, but it did not. Three years of "conventional" war followed, in which the United States provided the majority of soldiers to the UN forces in Korea. The war stopped in 1953, although there was never a peace treaty. Even today, the border between North and South Korea continues to be a possible trouble spot.

In the 1950s, there was a feeling in the United States as if the country were under attack. Communism seemed to be making gains everywhere. The United States and 10 countries of Western Europe formed **NATO** (North Atlantic Treaty Organization) to defend themselves against the Soviet Union. But military strength alone couldn't completely calm American fears.

What about communists closer to home? **Joseph McCarthy**, a United States senator from Wisconsin, played on these fears. For four years, McCarthy claimed that communists were working inside the United States, trying to break down the American system of government and American society. A Senate committee looked into the lives and backgrounds of government workers. Businesses, colleges, and even Hollywood searched their ranks for "communist sympathizers." In 1954, while investigating communists in the U.S. Army, McCarthy went too far. Americans watching the hearings on television saw how McCarthy operated, and

Berlin

Following World War II, the United States, Britain, France, and the Soviet Union divided German territory four ways. The German capital city, Berlin, was in the Soviet zone. The four powers divided Berlin four ways as well. In June 1948, the Soviets closed off Berlin to the rest of the world by blocking road, rail, and river traffic. Food, fuel, and other necessities could not get into the city. The Soviets hoped to force the other three powers to give up the city. For a while, there was great fear of war. President Truman ordered airplanes to fly needed supplies into Berlin. The Berlin Airlift lasted nearly a year before the Soviet Union lifted its blockade in 1949.

From 1949 to 1961, millions of people escaped Soviet control in East Germany by crossing from East Berlin to West Berlin. Then, the East German government built the Berlin Wall to keep people in. The wall stood for 28 years as a symbol of the Cold War. In 1989, as communist governments were collapsing all over Eastern Europe, the Berlin Wall also came down.

he began to lose support. But while it lasted, **McCarthyism** created a climate of fear in the United States. People were suspicious of their neighbors. Many lives and careers were ruined by accusations that turned out to be false.

Vietnam and Cuba

The closeness of China and the Soviet Union to Southeast Asia made it the focus of American anticommunist efforts after the Korean War. In the 1950s, the United States began helping a democratic government in **South Vietnam** in its struggle against communist **North Vietnam**. First the United States gave money; then, it sent military advisors, hoping to make the South Vietnamese army strong enough to defeat the communists on its own.

Not many Americans knew about Vietnam in the early 1960s. The building of the Berlin Wall kept the focus of anticommunist activity on Europe. Yet there also was growing communist activity only 90 miles off the Florida coast. In 1959, **Fidel Castro** overthrew the government of the island nation of **Cuba**. He announced that he was a communist and began looking for economic help from the Soviet Union.

The United States was not pleased with Castro's Cuba. In 1961, Cubans trained by the United States tried unsuccessfully to overthrow Castro. The **Bay of Pigs** invasion was a complete failure. Afterward, Cuba began building up its military force, fearing an American attack.

In October 1962, American spy planes discovered that the Soviet Union was putting nuclear weapons in Cuba. Missiles launched from Cuba could reach most of the east coast of the United States in minutes. President **John F. Kennedy** demanded that the missiles be removed. The Soviets refused, and for a few days, it seemed as if a world war was close. The Soviet Union backed down, however, and the **Cuban Missile Crisis** came to a peaceful end.

Once relations between the United States and Cuba

Cuba

cooled down, American leaders began to focus once again on Vietnam. In 1964, North Vietnamese troops attacked American ships off the coast of North Vietnam. Congress voted to allow President **Lyndon Johnson** to "prevent further aggression." Johnson began a huge military buildup in Vietnam. From 1965 to 1973, more than a million American soldiers served in Vietnam. Despite the large force, the United States could not defeat the North Vietnamese. A peace agreement was reached in 1973, and American troops went home. The United States hoped that the agreement would guarantee democracy in South Vietnam. It did not. In 1975, North Vietnam conquered the South and reunited the country under a Communist government.

Quick Review 3: How did the domino theory make Cuba a high priority for anticommunists?

_____

_____

_____

_____

End of the Cold War

After Vietnam, world events continued to be viewed as extensions of the Cold War. The periodic wars between Israel and its Arab neighbors, civil wars in the African country of Angola, and internal troubles in several Central American countries brought with them the risk of wider U.S.-Soviet conflict. American leaders, especially President **Richard Nixon**, worked to lessen tensions between the United States, China, and the Soviet Union. In 1972, Nixon, who had always been a strong opponent of communism, became the first U.S. president to visit China.

During the 1970s, the United States began cutting its military budgets. Leaders disagreed over whether this was a good idea. Some suggested that since tensions were fewer, there was less need for huge, expensive weapons systems. Others argued that the United States was still at risk and that high levels of spending should continue. When **Ronald Reagan** became president in 1981, he pushed higher levels of military spending through Congress. At the same time, he held several meetings with Soviet leader **Mikhail Gorbachev** to talk about reducing the nuclear threat.

A New Map

One of the outcomes of World War II was the end of the colonial system that had been a part of world history since the 1500s. Britain granted independence to India. The French were forced out of Southeast Asia. Other European colonies in Africa and Asia received their independence. The United States believed some of these newly independent countries were at risk of falling under communist influence.

Dwight Eisenhower, who had commanded Allied troops in Europe during World War II, was elected president in 1952. He saw the countries of the world as if they were a row of dominoes. "You knock over the first one, and what will happen to the last one is the certainty that it will go over very quickly." The American policy of containment was aimed at keeping the domino theory from becoming a reality.

John F. Kennedy

John F. Kennedy of Massachusetts was elected president in 1960. He was the second-youngest person ever to serve in the office. In his inaugural address, he challenged Americans to work hard against Cold War enemies and for the good of all Americans. "Ask not what your country can do for you," he said. "Ask what you can do for your country." Kennedy was an active anticommunist. He also supported the Civil Rights Movement. On November 22, 1963, Kennedy was assassinated in Dallas, Texas. His murder has been the subject of hundreds of conspiracy theories. Kennedy and his wife, Jacqueline, were a glamorous couple; however, his personal life, which was not reported on while he was alive, would have been the subject of great controversy if he were president today.

Most previous leaders of the Soviet Union had been older men who had been raised under the dictatorship of Joseph Stalin and who remembered the awful cost of World War II. Gorbachev was a different kind of leader. He was younger and more energetic. He had clearly watched American politicians at work and learned from them. And he tried to change the way the Soviet people lived. He tried to bring what he called *glasnost* (openness) to Soviet society, easing the dictatorship that had ruled their lives.

A little taste of openness proved to be the end of the Soviet Union and the communist system. The events that ended the 50-year Cold War had less to do with diplomats and presidents than with the actions of common people. In the late 1980s, Soviet-controlled governments in Eastern Europe collapsed as citizens demanded democracy and Communist governments found themselves unable to hold on to power. Communist leaders were forced out in Poland, East Germany, Czechoslovakia, Romania, and other countries that had been controlled by the Soviet Union since World War II. The border between East and West Berlin was opened, and the Berlin Wall came down. The Cold War was clearly reaching its end.

The Soviet Union itself was headed for the history books, too. When the United States led an international effort against Iraq in the 1991 **Persian Gulf War**, the Soviet Union was not an important part of it. One year later, the Soviet Union broke into 15 smaller countries. Each of them is still working to adjust to life without communism. Communists are still active in the largest of the former Soviet states, Russia. A return to some form of communist system there can't be ruled out. Voters might even choose it. Russia and the other republics have had less prosperous economies since the breakup than they had before. Some voters believe a return to communism might improve their standard of living.

Quick Review 4: How did Ronald Reagan deal with the Soviet Union during the 1980s?

_____

_____

_____

_____

Civil Rights

Americans like to remember the 1950s as a peaceful time when everyone lived in a nice house with a mother who stayed home and a father who went to work. We "remember" that there was no crime in the streets and no violence on TV, and that everyone was prosperous and happy.

It wasn't quite like that. The lifestyles of Americans changed greatly in the 1950s. Many families did move to suburbs and raise children, but not all. There were working mothers and single parent families. And if you happened to be African American, you were probably not welcome in the new suburbs. In the South, African Americans were restricted in where they could go, and in many places, laws made it nearly impossible for them to vote. Nearly 90 years after the Civil War, it was clear that some of the goals of the war had yet to be reached.

In 1954, the U.S. Supreme Court ruled that the practice of keeping separate-but-equal schools for black and white students was unconstitutional. The decision in the case of **Brown v. Board of Education of Topeka, Kansas**, meant that children of both races would be required to attend the same schools. Many Southern states fought school **desegregation**. In the most famous case, President Eisenhower sent federal soldiers to Little Rock, Arkansas, in 1957, to see that nine black students were allowed to enter their school building safely.

The **Civil Rights Movement** may have been born in 1955 on a bus in Montgomery, Alabama, when **Rosa Parks** refused to give up her seat to a white passenger as the law required. When she was arrested, black citizens of Montgomery stopped riding the buses for over a year, until the city changed its law. A young minister named **Martin Luther King, Jr.**, helped lead the bus boycott and became the movement's driving force.

For the next 13 years, King and others staged mostly peaceful protests to end desegregation and win voting rights. They were inspired by Gandhi, the leader of India, who believed peace was more effective than violence in causing change. Nevertheless, they were sometimes met with violence from whites opposed to them. On August 28, 1963, thousands of black Americans (and many white Americans, too) marched in Washington, D.C. On that day, King gave his most famous speech. He explained the purpose of the March on Washington and outlined his dream for what America would one day be.

> *I have a dream my four little children will one day live in a nation where they will not be judged by the color of their skin, but by the content of their character.*
>
> —**Martin Luther King, Jr.**, August 28, 1963

King continued to work for equal rights. With the support of Presidents Kennedy and Johnson, federal civil rights and voting rights acts were passed in Congress to ensure that state laws could not restrict the rights of citizens. Near the end of his life, King was criticized by other African American leaders for going too slowly instead of demanding immediate action.

On April 4, 1968, King was in Memphis, Tennessee, supporting striking city workers. He was shot dead while standing on the balcony of his motel room. A white man, **James Earl Ray**, was convicted of the crime.

Quick Review 5: What were some of the goals of the Civil Rights Movement?

_____

_____

_____

The Women's Movement

Women were another group struggling for equality, especially in the 1960s and 1970s. Young women born after World War II were not willing to live the kind of lives their mothers and grandmothers had lived. Many felt limited by the options society seemed to give them. The women's movement tried to educate women and encourage them to go beyond what was expected of them. The movement also argued for equal pay for equal work and tried to amend the Constitution to guarantee equal rights. The Equal Rights Amendment failed, but the women's movement was successful in changing attitudes about the role of women in society.

Scandal

In 1972, Republican President Richard Nixon planned to run for reelection. Some of his assistants decided to break into the headquarters of the Democratic National Committee, which was located in Washington's **Watergate** office building. Most historians believe Nixon did not know about the break-in before it happened, but it seems clear that when he found out, he worked to cover it up.

The Watergate scandal lasted two years. Many of Nixon's assistants went to jail. The House of Representatives held impeachment hearings into Nixon's conduct, just as it did with President Clinton in 1998. Impeachment did not go as far in 1974 as it did in 1998. The House Judiciary Committee approved articles of impeachment against Nixon, but before the full House could vote on them, Nixon resigned from office.

The Watergate scandal changed American life and politics. Before Watergate, Americans usually trusted their leaders to do what was right. After Watergate, politicians no longer received such trust automatically. The news media had played an important part in uncovering the scandal. After Watergate, instead of simply reporting on what government and its leaders did, reporters began looking for evidence of scandals in the making.

New Millennium

Life itself is a challenge, so it's not news that the United States faces new challenges heading into the new millennium. At home, we continue to fight violent crime and drug use, although the good news in the late 1990s was that the rates of both had begun to fall. The economy was strong through most of the '90s, but history shows that economies cannot grow indefinitely. At some point, we will have to deal with a slowdown.

American politics became very rough in the 1990s. Instead of viewing one another as fellow Americans with differing points of view, Republicans and Democrats often looked at one another as enemies with threatening ideas who had to be stopped. It's doubtful that the United States can deal with its other challenges in such a political environment, but changing it will be a difficult process.

Beyond our borders, Americans can no longer look at the world with a Cold War view. Security no longer equals keeping one enemy at bay. The United States will continue to encourage freedom and democracy everywhere, but it's hard to tell what direction the next challenge will come from. Terrorists can strike anywhere. Chemical and biological weapons can be difficult to stop. And although the nuclear stand off of the Cold War is over, there are still many nuclear weapons in the world, and they're still dangerous.

> *Some really believe that after the Cold War, the United States can play a secondary role in the world . . . just as some made sure we did after World War I. But if you look at the results from Bosnia to Haiti, from the Middle East to Northern Ireland, it proves once again that American leadership is indispensable.*
>
> —**Bill Clinton**, 1995

Up Close:

At Home in the '60s and '70s

Like any other 20-year period in history, the 1960s and 1970s had their share of major events, such as the Kennedy and King assassinations, the 1969 landing on the moon by American astronauts, Nixon's resignation, and the taking of American hostages by Iran in 1979. Yet what people who lived through these decades often remember best is the **popular culture**: clothes, music, TV shows, and movies.

In the 1960s, clothing could be a symbol of who you were. Young people who disagreed with the way American life was going often tried to dress in ways that made their feelings clear. They wore wild colors and strange accessories much different from what people in "the establishment" were wearing. By the 1970s, "dressing up" was back in style, but colors were still unusual. Non-natural fibers, such as polyester, were popular.

Above: *Singers Joan Baez and Bob Dylan performed at the Civil Rights March on Washington in 1963.*

Music was extremely important to people growing up in the 1960s. Performers often sang about political issues such as war and poverty. By the 1970s, people were growing tired of such "serious" music. Disco asked you to dance, not think; punk rock got angry about the world the '60s generation had made, but didn't have any answers for it.

In the 1960s, TV and movies did not reflect the real world. Hollywood had changed little since the 1930s. On TV, most of the faces were white and middle class. In the 1970s, movie studios discovered that young people would pay to see more serious films, at least until *Star Wars* proved that big-screen comic books would be the most popular films of all. TV producers learned that real people would watch programs that were based on real life. By the end of the 1970s, cable was bringing more channels and choices into American homes. Viewers were just beginning to feel the power of television.

What Do You Think?

Directions: Answer the questions on the lines provided. Be prepared to discuss your answers in class.

1. Why did World War II leave the United States as the world's most powerful country?

   _____

   _____

   _____

   _____

   _____

2. Some historians suggest that Cold War tensions may have kept small wars from getting out of control. How could this be?

   _____

   _____

   _____

   _____

   _____

   _____

   _____

   _____

   _____

Test Your Knowledge

Directions: Choose three items from the list. Imagine that you are writing a short encyclopedia entry for each one. Include the basic information a reader would have to know in order to begin understanding the person, place, or event, including time, location, details of the events, and what happened as a result of them. You may use outside research materials and additional sheets of paper if necessary.

Berlin

Containment

Cuban Missile Crisis

End of the Cold War

Hiroshima

Holocaust

Joseph McCarthy

Korean War

Manhattan Project

Martin Luther King, Jr.

Vietnam War

Watergate

_____

_____

_____

_____

_____

_____

_____

_____

_____

_____

_____

_____

_____

_____

Unit 2 Review Test

1. In the 1880s and 1890s, patterns of immigration to the United States changed. Where did most immigrants during this time come from?

    A. Asia

    B. Africa

    C. southern and eastern Europe

    D. northern and western Europe

2. All of the following have been reasons for immigration to the United States. Which one was the most important reason between about 1880 and 1910?

    A. food shortages

    B. religious persecution

    C. desire for gold

    D. economic opportunity

Directions: Read the passage, then use it to answer Numbers 3 and 4.

Life in *The Jungle*

Upton Sinclair was born into a lower middle-class family in Baltimore, Maryland. His early writing had heroes fighting against social problems. In 1904, he was hired to write a book about the difficult lives of workers in American industries. Sinclair went to Chicago and lived with the stockyard workers. His descriptions of the unsafe and unsanitary working conditions in the meat industry led to changes in how the whole food industry operated. He called his book *The Jungle*. "I aimed for the public's heart," the author noted, "and I hit it in the stomach."

3. Upton Sinclair can be best described as a

    A. muckraker.

    B. working man.

    C. political leader.

    D. management expert.

4. Which group would be most likely to demand changes in the meat-packing industry, based on Sinclair's book?

    A. labor

    B. capital

    C. consumers

    D. management

---

5. While he was president, Theodore Roosevelt used the "big stick" in all of these areas except

    A. building the Panama Canal.

    B. ruling the Philippine Islands.

    C. taking the United States into World War I.

    D. being the "policeman" of North and Central America.

6. Which statement best describes the attitude of Americans toward foreign policy during the 1920s and 1930s?

    A. Let Europe take care of itself and we'll take care of ourselves.

    B. The United States must make the world safe for democracy.

    C. The United States is the only country that can lead the world.

    D. If someone wants to attack us, we'll fight, but only if we are attacked.

7. The leading enemy of the United States in World War I was

    A. France.

    B. Mexico.

    C. Germany.

    D. Great Britain.

8. Which statement about the temperance movement is false?

    A. The movement was responsible for Prohibition.

    B. The movement started suddenly, right after World War I.

    C. The movement believed alcohol caused family problems.

    D. The movement's effects are still felt in some parts of America today.

Fight for the Right

Left: *In 1912, these women marched for voting rights in New York City.*

9. In 1920, the Nineteenth Amendment gave women the right to vote in national elections. Who or what had given them the right to vote in some other elections?

    A. the president

    B. public pressure

    C. Susan B. Anthony

    D. state constitutions

Crash

Directions: Read the paragraph, then use it to answer Number 10.

On Monday, October 21, prices started to fall quickly. Investors became fearful. Prices stabilized a little on Tuesday and Wednesday, but then, on Black Thursday, October 24, everything fell apart again. By this time, most major investors had lost confidence in the market. Once enough investors had decided the boom was over, it was over.

10. The paragraph describes
    A. the event that started World War II.
    B. an average week of stock market trading.
    C. the event that started the Great Depression.
    D. the event that led to the forming of the United Nations.

11. A great change brought about by the New Deal was
    A. the beginning of an appeasement policy in Europe.
    B. the forming of an international organization to stop wars.
    C. a smaller role for the president in leading the government.
    D. a stronger role for government in helping citizens directly.

12. How was President Franklin Roosevelt able to get around the Neutrality Acts and help European allies?
    A. by creating the Lend-Lease program with Churchill
    B. by tricking the Japanese into bombing Pearl Harbor
    C. by convincing Congress to declare war on Germany
    D. by drawing the Soviet Union into forming an alliance with Hitler

13. "Rosie the Riveter" was a symbol of what force during World War II?

    A. women working in film

    B. women fighting in battle

    C. women serving as nurses

    D. women working in industry

14. During the Cold War, many of the world's nations took sides with either the United States or the Soviet Union. If a country chose neither side, but still wanted to be involved in international affairs, to which group would it most likely belong?

    A. NATO

    B. the United Nations

    C. the Marshall Plan

    D. the League of Nations

15. Which list puts the events in the correct time order from earliest to latest?

    A. Kennedy assassination, Watergate, fall of the Berlin Wall, first atomic bomb

    B. Watergate, fall of the Berlin Wall, first atomic bomb, Kennedy assassination

    C. First atomic bomb, Kennedy assassination, Watergate, fall of the Berlin Wall

    D. fall of the Berlin Wall, Kennedy assassination, first atomic bomb, Watergate

16. Which of the following challenges is the United States least likely to face in the 21st century?

    A. terrorism

    B. communism

    C. political divisions

    D. economic difficulties

UNIT

3

Left: *Every day all over the world, people make economic decisions.*

Economics

When you have to make a decision, how do you do it? Homework or TV? Chocolate or vanilla? Boxers or briefs? How do you make up your mind?

People usually examine the choices they must make by analyzing costs and benefits. We ask ourselves how much are we willing to pay—in money, time, or something else—to get a certain level of benefit. Our goal is usually to get the maximum possible benefit. We don't always measure benefit in terms of money or goods. Sometimes we measure it by the way our decision makes us feel. No matter what, though, weighing costs and benefits are what our lives are all about.

Weighing costs and benefits is an economic activity. It's possible to say—and some people have—that we are economic creatures first and foremost. This unit is about the many ways we economic creatures make decisions, the many tools we use to make decisions, and the many ideas at work behind our decisions.

Lesson 13

Economic Concepts

Economics is the study of the ways people divide a limited amount of resources to meet their wants and needs, which can be unlimited. If you have studied economics in any detail, however, you know that beneath that simple definition is a complex science with many interlocking concepts. This lesson will attempt to sort them out.

It will help you to think of economics as having two branches:

- **Microeconomics** is the study of the parts of an economy, including such factors as prices, markets, industries, and so on.

- **Macroeconomics** is the study of an economy as a whole, including production, inflation, unemployment, and other factors.

Dr. Orley Amos, a professor of economics at Oklahoma State University, describes the difference by saying macroeconomics is the study of the forest, while microeconomics is the study of the trees. (Dr. Amos's Internet site, *AmosWorld*, is one of the best sites on the Web for useful information on economics. It's definitely not dry, boring, textbook stuff. Visit *AmosWorld* at http://amos.bus.okstate.edu.)

Consumption

Consumption refers to the goods and services bought by households for personal use. When you buy groceries or clothes, you are consuming goods. When you have your shoes repaired or get a tattoo, you are consuming services. All of these (even the services, for purposes of this explanation) can be called **consumption goods**. Most of these goods are used up in a relatively short period of time. You'll have to buy more groceries next week, and you'll buy new shoes now and then (although that tattoo is there to stay).

Businesses also buy goods and services. They do so for one reason only: to help the business create more goods and services to sell. These purchases fall into two categories: **inventory goods** and **investment** or **capital goods**. Inventory goods will be sold to consumers at a later time. When a clothing store buys a new shipment of sweaters, the sweaters are inventory goods. Investment goods go directly toward helping the business create new goods and services. When the tattoo parlor buys some big new needles, those are investment goods. It's an investment in the future growth of the business.

Both inventory goods and investment goods help businesses do whatever it is they do. Investment goods are usually expected to last longer than consumption goods. Inventory goods are used up faster than investment goods.

When taken together across the entire economy, the total sales value of consumption, inventory, and investment goods purchases equals the **Gross Domestic Product**, or **GDP** for short. The GDP of the United States is the total value of goods and services produced by the American economy, whether it is produced by American companies or by foreign companies doing business in the United States. GDP figures are usually released on a quarterly basis (every three months). As you might expect, the numbers are very large. For example, the GDP for the first quarter of 1998 was more than 8.5 trillion dollars. Over a whole year, that's nearly 34 trillion dollars.

Households, individuals or groups who buy consumption goods, are only one **sector**, or part of the economy. Buyers of investment goods, **businesses**, make up another sector. A third important sector is **government**. Its purchases are similar to those made by households and businesses, but also somewhat different.

The government buys goods and services for its own use, much like households do. An example of such a short-term, repeated expense for government is the salaries of teachers and police officers. The government also spends its money on longer-lasting goods, such as roads and bridges. These expenses do not help make more money, in the way expenses for investment goods help businesses make money. Yet they are examples of a similar kind of expense. Both of these government expenses are counted in the GDP.

The government makes a third kind of indirect contribution to GDP known as a **transfer payment**. These payments include Social Security, welfare, and other spending for social purposes. Nothing is produced or consumed directly by these payments, so they don't count toward the nation's GDP. When the people who receive the payments spend the money, however, it will be.

One other economic statistic goes into calculating the GDP. Imports and exports—goods and services bought and sold from foreign sources—are also totaled up. If the United States sells more abroad than it buys, the figure is added to the GDP. If it buys more from foreign countries than it sells, which is what has happened most often in recent years, the figure is subtracted.

GDP or GNP?

Gross National Product, or GNP, is very similar to GDP. GNP includes all goods and services produced by American companies no matter where they are located. It doesn't count goods and services produced by foreign companies on American soil. For example, the output of a Japanese-owned car factory located in the United States would count in the GDP but not in the GNP. On the other hand, the output of an American-owned computer factory located in Mexico would count in the GNP but not the GDP. Usually, there's only about a one-percent difference between GNP and GDP. Although the two terms mean almost the same thing, Gross Domestic Product is the preferred term.

The GDP is a broad indicator of a country's economic activity. It's most useful for showing the general health of an economy. You'll read about other economic indicators later in this lesson.

Quick Review 1: What does the Gross Domestic Product figure show?

_____

_____

_____

Name the three sectors of the American economy.

_____

_____

_____

Where It Happens

All this buying and selling we've been talking about happens in the **marketplace**, or **market**. It's not a physical place you can visit, although shops, stores, and malls are part of it. Economists define the market as the sum of buyers and sellers of any good or service and their interaction. Therefore, the marketplace can be as broad as the entire American economy or as limited as the market for baseball cards, bicycle parts, or body piercing.

Everything that is exchanged from a buyer to a seller has a **price**. One way of defining price is to call it an agreement between the buyer and the seller on what something is worth. It really is an agreement, although it might not seem like one. Imagine that you go to a clothing store and see a pair of jeans you like. The price is $59.95. Chances are good that the clerk won't agree to take $40 for them instead. But if many, many customers refuse to pay $59.95, the seller of the jeans may have to lower the price to get people to buy.

Supply and demand also have a lot to do with price. In brief, the law of supply and demand explains why people will pay big bucks for that hard-to-find doll or toy at Christmas. The less of something there is, the more expensive it is likely to be.

That's not the only key to price, however. Visit an athletic shoe store and you'll see boxes and boxes of expensive shoes. There are plenty of shoes to be found, but the prices remain high. That's because shoe manufacturers have found a point at which consumers' desire for their product is equal to the amount consumers are willing to pay. Producers and sellers charge "what the market will bear." If they can't sell a product at the price they have set, they have two choices—either lower the price or find a way to increase the desire of consumers to buy it.

In a kind of market called **pure competition**, supply and demand is the only factor influencing price. In theory, everyone has an equal chance to get a fair share of resources.

Very few markets have pure competition. Instead, the "real world" has **imperfect competition**. There are "winners" and "losers." Some people get their share, some get more, and some get less. Pure competition assumes an unlimited number of producers, but in the real world, the numbers are limited. In some markets, there is only one producer. For example, in most communities, you must buy your electric service from one company (although this is changing in some areas). The electric company has a **monopoly**. Pure competition also assumes that consumers have perfect information about the goods they can buy. This is not the case in the real world, where advertising has a great influence and may provide imperfect information.

In addition, most major economies around the world have government regulations that affect both supply and price. Price can also have an effect on supply and demand, instead of the other way around. To sum up: Most major world economies are examples of imperfect competition.

Quick Review 2: How does the marketplace offer incentives to buyers and sellers?

_____

_____

_____

_____

_____

Why It's Worth It to Work Hard

Scarcity is basic to the study of economics. Because resources are limited but wants and needs are not, a basic problem of economics concerns who gets the resources. The law of supply and demand means that buyers who can afford to pay the price will often be able to get the goods, and those who cannot often will not. In this way, the market handles what economists call allocation of scarce goods and services.

There are other ways to allocate scarce goods. For example, a government agency could see that everyone receives an equal share of scarce goods and services, whatever they might be. Sound like a good idea? Well, think about it this way. Imagine you want the coolest sports car Detroit can make. If you have to earn the money to buy it, and you really, really want it, you will work hard to get it. But if everyone received a sports car on his or her 16th birthday, how hard would he or she work? When the market allocates scarce goods, people have an incentive to work harder than they would if scarce goods were distributed evenly. This is only bad news if you're not willing to work. If you are willing to work, there's no limit to what you can accomplish (almost).

The Flop of the Century

Markets not only determine what people will buy, but what people can sell. If you can't find someone to buy your product, it doesn't make any sense to produce it. One of the classic production mistakes of all time happened in the 1950s, when the Ford Motor Company produced a model called the Edsel. Ford spent millions designing and building it. When it was introduced, people laughed at it. Consumers didn't like the way it looked. In fact, they didn't like much about the Edsel at all, and they simply wouldn't buy it. In 1960, Ford quit making Edsels after three years. The case of the Edsel is an example of how consumers can have an impact on what producers make. People who bought Edsels are having the last laugh, though. Edsels have become valuable collector cars.

Economic Indicators

When you visit the doctor, he or she checks several indicators of your health, such as your weight, your temperature, and your blood pressure. These indicators help the doctor to know how healthy you are. **Economic indicators** serve a similar purpose. By looking at economic indicators, economists can tell how healthy an economy is. You've already read about GDP, but it's just one of the major indicators.

Consumer Price Index

The **inflation rate** is an indication of how fast prices are rising. (You'll read more about inflation later in this lesson.) The rate is a measure of change in the **Consumer Price Index (CPI)**, which is published monthly. The CPI is an index of the prices of 400 goods and services sold across the country, in categories such as housing, food, transportation, clothing, and medical care. When the U.S. Bureau of Labor Statistics publishes the CPI, it shows not only an overall indication of the rate of inflation in the economy, but the rate of inflation in each category.

The raw numbers of the CPI are not especially important, and you'll almost never see or hear them reported in the media. (In November 1998, for example, the index stood at 164.0.) Instead, the interesting numbers are the overall rate of inflation and the rates in the different categories, which refer to the percent increase over a specific time, usually a month.

Above: *In the late 1950s, the Ford Motor Company spent millions designing and marketing the Edsel. It was a flop, although the people who bought them are having the last laugh. Today, Edsels are valuable collector cars.*

Consumer Price Index, November 1998

Item	Change From October 1998 (percent)	Change From November 1997 (percent, unadjusted)
Food and Beverages	0.2	1.5
Housing	0.2	2.3
Apparel	0.3	2.3
Transportation	0.0	0.2
Medical Care	0.2	3.5
Recreation	0.2	1.3
Education and Communication	0.2	1.0
Other Goods and Services	-0.3	4.6
All Items	0.2	1.5

Source: *Bureau of Labor Statistics*

This table shows that the inflation rate for food and beverages was 0.2 percent in November 1998. For a whole year (November 1997 through November 1998), food and beverage prices increased by about 1.5 percent. Note that prices in the category of "other goods and services" actually went down in November 1998, but for the year, they were up 4.6 percent.

CPI numbers are broken down within each category. Note that inflation was extremely low in the transportation category: only 0.2 percent for the year. This is because average gasoline prices fell nearly 12 percent in 1998 until they were almost 25 percent lower than the 1990 prices. Inflation in the education and communication category was also very low, thanks to a 34.4 percent drop in the average cost of personal computers, monitors, printers, and other equipment during 1998.

The figures in the far-right column are unadjusted. Normally, the CPI is **seasonally adjusted** to account for price differences that depend on the season of the year. (Some fruits and vegetables cost less in the summer and more in the winter, for example.) For the first 11 months of 1998 (January through November), the seasonally adjusted CPI was 1.6 percent. Because economists believe that inflation can be as high as 2.5 percent in a healthy economy, the rate of inflation for 1998 was quite low.

The CPI (formerly known as the **Cost-of-Living Index**) is used to determine cost-of-living adjustments in Social Security payments, federal retirement benefits, and some union contracts. People who receive these payments get increases based on the inflation rate as shown by the CPI. For the rest of America, the CPI is a useful indicator of what things cost.

Quick Review 3: Not counting "other goods and services," which category of the CPI showed the largest increase between November 1997 and November 1998?

Interest Rates and Inflation

Interest rates represent the price of borrowed money. The higher interest rates are, the more expensive it is to borrow. Interest rates have a major impact on the American economy. Therefore, the level of interest rates can be an economic indicator.

When people have a lot of money to spend, prices tend to rise. The reason is that when there is a lot of money moving in the economy, the demand for goods usually goes up. As demand for goods rises, it puts pressure on the supply of goods. Production may be unable to keep up with demand. Therefore, prices for what is available usually rise. This is **inflation**. Some inflation is normal, but rapid inflation is bad for the economy. If prices rise faster than income, that means people and businesses can buy less. Businesses are more expensive to operate, and it becomes harder for them to sell their goods and services.

One way to control inflation is to cut the amount of money people have to spend. The federal government does this through control of interest rates. If interest rates go up, it makes money more expensive. People and businesses are less likely to borrow. Higher interest rates cut the **money supply** in the economy. Such cuts can help hold down inflation.

In the same way, lower interest rates can boost the economy. If money is less expensive, more people and businesses will borrow, increasing the money supply. Yet it can be dangerous to increase the money supply too greatly because—you guessed it—inflation could begin to speed up.

Deflation, meaning rapidly falling prices, is the opposite of inflation. How can falling prices possibly be a bad thing? If prices fall too far, businesses have a harder time making money, and workers lose their jobs. This can lead to broader economic troubles, and even to a recession or depression.

Interest rates are controlled by the **Federal Reserve**, or "Fed." The Fed is a banking network with several functions. Federal Reserve banks regulate commercial banks to make sure they are following banking laws. If a commercial bank doesn't have enough money to make payments to depositors, the Federal Reserve will loan money to cover the payments. The Federal Reserve also handles the money when commercial banks do business with each other. It processes checks and holds deposits for the U.S. Department of the Treasury and other government agencies.

The most important job of the Federal Reserve System in the United States is, however, to control the money supply. The Fed controls the money supply by setting certain interest rates. Because the money supply has such a large impact on the economy as a whole, business and government leaders carefully watch the Federal Reserve for signals on what it may do with interest rates. The chairman of the Fed appears regularly before committees in Congress to give forecasts of future economic conditions.

Government, Budgets, and the Economy

Government is a major player in the American economy. (For purposes of this discussion, think of "the government" as every level all together: federal, state, and local.) Government spending accounts for about 20 percent of GDP. As you have already read, government spends its money in ways similar to households and businesses. Governments make repeated, short-term expenditures similar to household spending on consumer goods. They also make long-term, one-time expenditures on items similar to the investment goods bought by businesses.

Americans pay close attention to the federal **budget**, the amount of income and expenditures the government expects to have in a given year. From the late 1960s through the late 1990s, the federal budget ran at a **deficit**. The federal government spent more money than it took in and was forced to borrow the difference. Many Americans demanded that the budget be balanced, so that spending would be equal to income, or perhaps even less than income. Some even suggested that the Constitution be amended to require a **balanced budget**, so that it would be against the law for the United States to borrow a single dime to run the government.

Many economists suggest that **deficit spending** can be good for the country. Among other things, deficit spending helped

Borrowing and Spending

People in favor of a balanced budget say that it doesn't make sense for the government to spend money it doesn't have—yet American households and businesses do it all the time. When Americans buy a house, for example (which is an investment good), they don't pay for it out of the cash they have on hand. Instead, they borrow the money. When a company decides to buy new machinery or expand a factory, it usually pays for the expansion by borrowing the money as well. Borrowing to buy investment goods is considered a sensible practice, so long as a household or business can pay the money back.

A house is an investment good purchased by a household. We don't pay for our houses out of ready cash. Why do we expect our government to do so? If it makes good sense for a business to borrow the money to build a new factory, doesn't it make sense for the federal government to borrow for a road or a bridge—a similar kind of long-lasting investment expenditure?

The difference between short-term, repeated expenditures and long-term expenditures is often ignored in discussions of government spending. Do we have a spending problem, or is it an accounting problem? What do you think?

pay for the military might the United States needed to defeat Germany and Japan in World War II. Deficit spending can give the economy a boost during a slowdown. If the Constitution were to be amended to forbid deficit spending, the United States might not be able to meet such emergencies in the future.

There are good arguments against deficit spending, too. For one thing, the United States already owes trillions of dollars in debt. Even in an economy as large as ours, that's a mighty scary credit-card bill. In fact, around 20 percent of the federal budget each year is spent on interest payments alone. There was a time when this was less troublesome than it is now. The federal government borrows money by selling **treasury bonds**. When American citizens owned most of the bonds, the interest money stayed in the American economy. Today, more and more of the bonds are owned by foreign investors, so the interest money is flowing out of the American economy.

Quick Review 4: Briefly define each of the following terms.

Balanced budget: _____

_____

_____

_____

Deficit spending: _____

_____

_____

_____

What Do You Think?

Directions: Answer the questions on the lines provided. Be prepared to discuss your answers in class.

1. Why are there winners and losers in a competitive economy?

_____

_____

_____

_____

_____

_____

_____

2. Spending on consumption goods makes up about twice as much of the GDP as spending on investment goods. Economists say, however, that spending on investment goods is the engine that drives the economy. Why do they say this?

_____

_____

_____

_____

_____

_____

_____

Test Your Knowledge

Directions: Explain the similarities and differences between each pair of terms shown.

1. Consumption goods/Investment goods

   _____

   _____

   _____

   _____

   _____

   _____

2. Gross Domestic Product/Consumer Price Index

   _____

   _____

   _____

   _____

   _____

   _____

3. Inflation/Deflation

   _____

   _____

   _____

   _____

   _____

   _____

Directions: Match the definition to the correct term. Not all terms will be used.

4. _____ study of the parts of an economy

5. _____ government payments for Social Security, welfare, and other social programs

6. _____ another name for a reason to work hard

7. _____ a market with only one producer

8. _____ the price of borrowed money

9. _____ central banking network that regulates commercial banks, handles government funds, and controls money supply

10. _____ sold to investors by the federal government as a source of money

    A. microeconomics
    B. incentive
    C. inflation
    D. interest rate
    E. monopoly
    F. pure competition
    G. Federal Reserve
    H. treasury bonds
    I. macroeconomics
    J. inventory goods
    K. transfer payments

Lesson 14

Economic History

The history of economics probably goes back to the first primitive human being who traded something he or she had for something he or she wanted. This trading system, **barter**, is still in use today. Primitive societies use it, but so do children in school cafeterias who don't like what's packed in their lunches.

Today, the use of money drives our economies. Our societies have built many systems based on getting money and using it. This lesson is about money and those systems.

The History of Money

Most money has little value in and of itself. The materials used to make a $100 bill are worth a few cents at the most. The $100 bill has a greater value only because we *agree* that it does. There's nothing special about green ink on white paper. Anything can be a **medium of exchange** as long as people agree that it has value. **Precious metals** such as gold and silver became preferred media of exchange fairly early in human history. They were beautiful to look at, they could be easily made into coins, bars, or other shapes, and they were scarce, which made them more valuable.

In ancient China, people used tools as a medium of exchange. If you wanted to buy something from another person, you could pay for it by giving the other person a tool. As years went by, the Chinese began using miniature tools made of bronze. These gradually evolved into coins.

A problem with barter is that people don't always agree on what barter goods are worth. Even precious metals would buy a greater or lesser amount of goods depending upon the quantity and quality of the metal. The **Lydians**, who lived in the Mediterranean region, usually get credit for making the first coins in the 600s B.C. Their coins became a convenient medium of exchange because they were all the same size and weight. There was no need to weigh or measure them to determine how much they were worth.

Early American colonists used barter goods for trade. They also used any foreign coins they could find, including English shillings, Spanish dollars, and coins from France and the Netherlands. Massachusetts was the first American colony to make its own silver coins, called pine-tree shillings and oak-tree shillings, beginning in 1652. It was against English law for the colonists to make coins, but the Massachusetts coins were used throughout the colonies for many years.

Although the Chinese used paper money in the 600s A.D., it was not widespread until Europeans began using it in the 1600s. The first use of paper money in North America was in 1685. Playing cards signed by the governor of French Canada could be used just like gold or silver coins. Massachusetts was the first colony to print paper money, beginning in 1690.

The idea that a piece of paper could have the same value as a quantity of gold or silver was slow to gain acceptance. For that reason, paper money was controversial in the early years of the United States. The federal government printed millions of dollars to fund the Revolutionary War, but by 1780, the **continentals** were almost worthless. From then on, most people preferred **hard currency** such as gold and silver. Banks and private companies, not the government, issued most of the paper money used in the United States well into the 1800s. The federal government didn't begin printing large amounts of paper money again until the 1860s, to help fund the Civil War.

Quick Review 1: Why would people be reluctant to accept paper money?

_____

_____

_____

_____

_____

Feudalism

Different systems have grown up throughout history to provide basic economic organization for societies. One of the earliest was **feudalism**. Feudalism was a barter-based system that served both as an economic arrangement and a system of government. It was common in China, but more so in Europe during the Middle Ages.

A feudal society was organized as if it were a great pyramid. At the top was a king; beneath the king were levels of lesser lords; at the very bottom were masses of common people known as **peasants** or **serfs**. The king was the legal owner of all the land in his kingdom. From the king, lesser lords received the right to live on and use land in exchange for

What Money Is

Money has three functions:

- **A medium of exchange**. This means simply that money can be traded for a wide variety of things.

- **A medium of account**. Money is used to give value to things. It allows us to say what something is worth. By doing so, we can compare the value of one thing to another.

- **A store of wealth**. Money can be put away for future use. The more money you have, the greater your wealth. (Gold, jewels, works of art, stocks and bonds, and real estate are other stores of wealth.)

service in the king's army and payment of some taxes. Relationships between the king and his **vassals** (lesser lords holding **fiefs**, or land rights) served as a system of government in the kingdom. The vassals saw that the king's laws were obeyed and helped defend the kingdom from outside threats. In the feudal system, land equaled wealth. Kings and vassals who controlled land were the wealthiest and most powerful members of society.

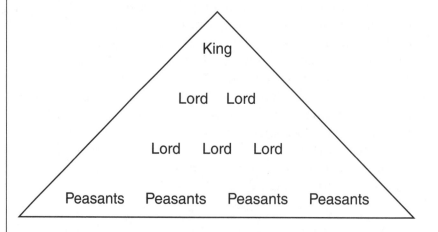

Right: *The feudal system was based on personal loyalties among kings and vassals. A king might grant a fief to one vassal, who would in turn grant fiefs to lesser vassals, and so on. There were often many levels between the top of the feudal pyramid and the bottom.*

At the bottom of the pyramid, the feudal system was more of an economic arrangement than a system of government, although it certainly limited what people on the bottom could and could not do. Peasants were permitted to live on land held by vassals. These peasants could raise animals and grow crops for themselves on the lord's land, but they were required to give the lord a share of their crops as rent. In addition, they were often obligated to spend some of their time working in the lord's fields. Several peasant families living in the same area made up a **manor**. The lord often lived in the manor house and permitted peasants to use some of his facilities, such as his ovens for baking bread or his barns for storing grain.

Peasants had few legal rights and little freedom of movement. They were required to serve whichever lord held the land on which they lived. If the land went to a different lord, they went with it. In some feudal societies, a peasant's possessions went to the lord at his death and not to his family.

Mercantilism

Feudalism worked well in an age of barter with only two well-defined socioeconomic classes. As societies and economies grew more complex during the Age of Exploration, the focus of economic systems shifted away from land to other forms of wealth. As countries such as Britain, France, and Spain began building prosperous colonies in the New World, they developed an economic system called **mercantilism**.

In the feudal system, land equaled wealth. In the mercantilist system, resources equaled wealth. The best way for a country to prosper was to import more products than it exported. To work effectively, mercantilism required centralized government control of economic activity. Colonies were a critical part of the system. They provided raw materials (and sometimes finished products) to their home countries. At the same time, colonies were required to purchase products made in the home countries.

Mercantilism thrived between about 1500 and 1750. It was driven by the growing spirit of **nationalism**, in which each country worked for its own best interest and against those of other countries if necessary. Most mercantilist countries increased their wealth greatly, but the wealth stayed with the upper and middle classes of citizens. The lowest class of citizens was expected to provide much of the labor that made the mercantilist system run, but they did not usually share in its benefits.

Capitalism

Near the end of the 17th century, philosopher **John Locke** wrote his *Second Treatise on Government*, which greatly influenced Thomas Jefferson and other leaders of the American Revolution with its ideas about the role of government and the rights of citizens. Locke's work also had an effect on economic history. He developed the concept of **private property**, which individuals had exclusive rights to control.

In 1776, British economist **Adam Smith** published *The Wealth of Nations*. Smith argued that the key to creating wealth was not mercantilism or land ownership, but the efforts of entrepreneurs using their private property. Smith believed that people should be free to make their own economic decisions. A whole society of individuals working to satisfy their self-interests, limited only by the self-interests of other individuals, would be most beneficial to the largest number of people. The role of government within such a system would be to protect property rights, but apart from that, Smith preferred to see people working without limitations. This **laissez-faire** policy (from a French phrase meaning "left alone") was attractive to those limited by what their mercantilist governments would permit them to do.

FAST FACT

Sometimes, mercantilism worked against the best interests of the colonies set up to benefit from the mercantilist system. For example, American colonists were required to buy most needed products from British manufacturers, even though other European manufacturers sometimes offered lower prices. Therefore, most mercantilist governments were forced to deal with smugglers who brought goods into colonies illegally.

The combination of private property and private individuals working freely in their own self-interests is basic to the system of **capitalism**. Private individuals use their wealth, or **capital**, in an attempt to make a **profit**. When a person is free to use his or her own resources, that person will use them in a way that tends to make the greatest profit. Therefore, capitalism is also known as **free enterprise**, or the **free enterprise system**.

Quick Review 2: In *The Wealth of Nations*, Adam Smith talked about "the invisible hand" that made capitalist economies run. What did he mean?

_____

_____

_____

_____

_____

Little "c" and Big "C"

Small "c" communism refers to the economic system described by Marx. Communism with a capital "C" refers to the system of government adopted by countries dominated by a communist party, such as the old Soviet Union, the People's Republic of China, and Cuba. All of these Communist governments claim (or claimed) to be working toward Marx's perfect state, yet in practice, they never get beyond the strict government control of the first stage. All aspects of economic, social, and political life are centrally controlled.

Communism

In the 19th century, **Karl Marx** developed **communism** as a critique of capitalism. Marx believed that it was the labor of workers, not the capital of investors, that created value. According to Marx, workers receive only a small part of that value in the form of wages, while the rest of the value goes to the capitalist. Workers, therefore, are not receiving their fair share. Marx urged workers to rise up and take control of the means of production for themselves. Marx saw all of human history as a series of economic struggles between classes. He believed that harmonious cooperation in the perfect communist economy would eliminate classes and the struggles between them altogether.

Such worker control would have two stages: during the **socialist** stage, the government would own and operate everything having to do with production, distribution, and consumption. Marx thought that the socialist stage would be temporary. It would oversee the transition to a perfect communist economy. Eventually, government control would no longer be necessary. In a perfect communist economy, everyone would work according to his of her ability and receive according to his of her needs.

While we often think of communism as being synonymous with repressive governments and threats to freedom, many countries friendly to freedom have adopted at least one element of Marx's theory. Countries such as Great Britain, Germany, Sweden, Norway, Denmark, Australia, and New Zealand have adopted some socialist ideas. In those countries, the government owns some large industries. These include utility companies, railroads, coal mines, and steel mills. Private individuals and companies control less-critical manufacturing industries, agriculture, and service industries.

In recent years, there has been a trend toward **privatization** of previously socialized industries, especially in Britain. Private ownership of such companies leads to greater profitability and lower prices for consumers.

Quick Review 3: Why would a socialist believe that government control of electric utilities is good for society?

_____

_____

_____

_____

_____

Mixed Economies

In practice, most economies—even the American economy—are neither purely capitalist nor purely socialist. Instead, they are **mixed economies**. For example, the idea of **regulated capitalism** evolved in the early 20th century. While people are mostly free to work in their self-interests, they are not *completely* free. Governments have taken on the power to regulate business. They can ensure fair competition, discourage monopoly, prohibit the sale of unsafe products, or limit wages and working hours.

China, which retains a Communist government, is permitting some experimentation with private ownership and competitive business. The former Soviet Union is struggling to find an effective system to replace its old Communist economy. It seems clear that Russians want a system that will incorporate some of the old ways along with a new, mostly free-market system.

Economic Systems

System	Source of Wealth	Role of Government in the Economy	Economic Decision Making	Economic Classes	Important Historical Concepts
Feudalism	Land or agriculture	Command economy, ruled by a king; small-scale markets in local areas	Centralized in the hands of the king's government	Upper (aristocracy); lower (peasants, servants)	Development of nation-states; acquiring land for colonies
Mercantilism	Resources, goods, services	Command economy, ruled by a king and/or his ministers; small-scale markets in local areas	Centralized in the hands of the king's government	Upper (aristocracy); middle (merchants); lower (farmers, laborers)	Colonialism and imperialism; increasing wealth by increasing colonial power
Capitalism	Capital from mercantile trade, used to invest in factories and for the sale of goods and services	Protects property rights; no role in setting priorities	Decentralized in the hands of private individuals acting in their own self-interests	Upper (large business and factory owners); middle (smaller business owners, merchants); lower (farmers, factory workers)	Industrial Revolution; factory system; entrepreneurship and private ownership of business
Socialism/ Communism	Equal sharing of wealth, by forced redistribution if necessary	Command economy or public control through government regulation	Controlled by government acting in the public interest (in theory; in practice, communist governments tend to define the public interest as they see fit)	None (in theory; in practice, communist systems have a small, privileged upper class made up mostly of government officials)	Several variations (Marxism is one); although some totalitarian countries tried to implement a socialist economy, no pure communist state ever existed
Mixed Economies	Source of wealth varies by country, but involves goods and services; limited equalizing of wealth	Mixture of capitalism and socialism; for example, regulated capitalism; government has some power to control privately owned businesses	Combination of private individuals acting in their own self-interests and public regulation	Number of classes depends on level of taxation and extent of government social programs	Role of multinational corporations with no fixed homeland; global economy

According to communist theory, no person should be wealthier than any other person. If you have more than your neighbor, you should give some to your neighbor so that you both have the same amount. Regulated capitalism doesn't go that far. Regulated capitalism recognizes that though there will be winners and losers in the economy, steps should be taken to limit the differences. This can be done by redistributing income from the wealthy to the less wealthy through taxation and welfare programs.

War—Hot and Cold

Full-scale wars usually require the population of a country at war to devote as much energy as possible to fighting, in hopes of winning. Such wars can't help but have a huge impact on the economies of the countries involved. There is a huge demand for war-related goods and services that must be met somehow. In most cases, this demand is met through higher taxes. Governments charge their citizens more to pay for the supplies and equipment needed to fight.

Taxes are usually not enough, however. In both World War I and World War II, the United States government raised money by selling **war bonds**. After the war, buyers of war bonds would get their money back with interest. The sales of these bonds and the high demand for goods increase the money supply in an economy. As you read in Lesson 13, an increased money supply usually leads to inflation—a general rise in prices. Higher levels of employment and a lower supply of consumer goods and services are also factors in sparking inflation. Every major participant in every major war has faced such inflation.

Following World War II, the United States moved into the Cold War. Although it wasn't a full-scale shooting war, it had a similar economic effect. Meeting the needs of the military buildup required tax increases. It kept employment levels high. Demand for consumer goods, which had been held down by World War II, exploded along with the population, thanks to the baby boom and the need to provide for young families.

While the United States economy stayed on a war footing, American leaders also declared war on poverty. The 1960s saw a great expansion of social programs to help less-fortunate people. The continuing strength of the American economy meant that large amounts of tax money were still coming in to spend. When the United States became deeply involved in an expensive war in Vietnam, however, the economy began to struggle. There wasn't enough money to fund social programs and a war without a tax increase, yet the government resisted raising taxes. Instead, it began borrowing billions each year. For the next 30 years, such deficit spending was a normal way of doing business.

In the early 1970s, the economy slowed further. Inflation grew to record levels as prices rose much faster than the incomes of workers. It was clear that the long expansion that benefited most Americans following World War II was over. Although the economy recovered in the 1980s, a much smaller percentage of the population profited from the recovery.

What Do You Think?

Directions: Answer the question on the lines provided. Be prepared to discuss your answer in class.

In the 20th century, command economies have tended to work in the short run but have been less effective in the long run. Name some reasons why this is true.

_____

_____

_____

_____

_____

_____

_____

_____

_____

Test Your Knowledge

Directions: Answer the question on the lines provided. You may use an additional sheet of paper if necessary.

Trace the idea of private property through the following economic systems: feudalism, mercantilism, capitalism, and communism. Questions you may wish to answer include: Who could own property? What was its role? How would those without property assess the economic system?

_____

_____

_____

_____

_____

_____

_____

_____

_____

_____

_____

_____

_____

_____

Lesson 15

Economic Life

So far in this unit, you have read about basic economic concepts and some economic history. In this lesson, you will read about some ways in which economics enters into your life on a daily basis.

Making Deals

A **contract** is a legal agreement between two **parties** (people or businesses) that tells what each person will do as part of a contract. For example, think about a pro athlete named Rod Rebound. Rod wants to play for the NBA's Washington Wizards. Rod and the team will sign a contract. The Wizards promise to pay Rod a certain amount of money for the season. In return, Rod promises to show up for practice every day and catch the team plane on time.

The purpose of a contract is to make sure both parties understand exactly what is expected of them. It's better to have an agreement in writing than to trust a **verbal** (spoken) agreement. After all, people sometimes remember conversations differently. If both parties read and sign the contract, there's no doubt later about what the agreement means.

A contract can spell out what will happen if either party violates it. For example, Rod's contract with the Wizards might say that if he misses practice, he has to pay a fine to charity. In some cases, the parties might disagree over whether a contract has been violated. If that happens, the dispute may have to be decided in court.

Contracts can be legally **enforced**. Imagine that Rod misses practice. The team takes Rod's fine money out of his next paycheck. Now, Rod claims the team has violated the contract by paying him less than it agreed to. But if he goes to court to get the fine money back, chances are good that he'll be told that the contract is enforceable. The team has a legal right to take fine money out of Rod's check.

There are other kinds of legal agreements involved when people make deals with one another. When you purchase a product, chances are it comes with a guarantee, a warranty, or both.

- A **guarantee** promises that the product will do what it says it will do. Guarantees often include a promise to give the buyer something if the product fails to live up to the guarantee. "Miracle Detergent is guaranteed to get mud stains out of lace curtains, or your money back."

- A **warranty** tells who has the responsibility for repairing or replacing the product and for how long. For example, carmakers will often promise to pay for certain repairs for three years or 30,000 miles. After three years or 30,000 miles, the owner of the car must pay for those repairs.

Credit

Businesses and consumers borrow money all the time. There's nothing wrong with doing that. It can make good financial sense to borrow money to buy a car, a house, or a business. Banks are in the business of helping people get the things they want and need by loaning money to borrowers.

Before a bank will loan money, it wants to be sure it will get the money back someday. The bank will check the **credit rating** of a person or business asking for a loan. To keep a good credit rating, it's important to pay your bills, and to pay them on time. A person with a good credit rating can get a loan more easily than someone with a bad rating. That person also can get a bigger loan.

Buying on **credit** is a form of borrowing. Instead of paying $14,298.73 for that new car all at once, you might pay only $2,000 now and promise to pay the rest over the next five years, a little each month. If you choose to do this, you will pay more than the total cost of the car. You also will pay **interest**. As you read in Lesson 13, interest is the cost of borrowed money, expressed as a percentage. If the interest rate on your car loan is 8 percent, that means you will pay 8 percent of the balance due each year in interest charges.

Using a credit card is also a form of borrowing money. When you buy clothing on credit, the credit card company pays the clothing store; you pay the credit card company. As is the case with other loans, the credit card company charges you interest for the right to use their money.

Credit card interest rates can be incredibly high. Some credit cards charge as much as 22 percent interest. If you charge $100 on a card and leave the balance alone for a year, you will have to pay back $122. The more you charge, the more dollars of interest you pay.

The Credit Card Company Doesn't Want You to Read This Box

Most credit card companies don't require you to pay back all your charges at once. They don't want you to. The longer it takes you to pay off the card, the more interest you are charged and the more money the card company makes. The interest goes right back onto the card, which means that after a while, you're paying interest on interest.

Because credit cards are so easy to get, the average American family has several of them. The average family also has thousands of dollars charged to them. A $5,000 balance at 20 percent means $1,000 per year in interest, which is a big bite out of a family's income. Think of what you can buy for $1,000.

Credit cards are a useful tool. On vacation or business trips, when people don't want to carry large sums of cash, a credit card is helpful. Yet more and more people are using them for everyday purchases, such as groceries, fast food, and gasoline. Cards are convenient, but consumers don't often think about the interest they'll have to pay . . . and pay . . . and pay.

Quick Review 1: Why is a good credit rating important to a person's financial future?

_____

_____

_____

Investments

Investments make money grow. Many people put money away in a bank to use at some future time. Banks pay interest to savers, so the longer your money stays in the bank, the more interest you will receive. Because banks loan money to people in their communities who need it, saving at a bank is a way of investing in your community. Bank saving is a very safe investment.

There are other types of investments. You can invest your money in a business. Imagine that your neighbor Ellie wants to start a flower shop. You've seen Ellie grow flowers in her garden, and you know her shop will be a success. But there's a problem: Ellie doesn't have enough money to start the business by herself. Because you believe in her, you give Ellie some of your money to start the business. You are an **investor** in the flower shop. After the shop gets going, Ellie may choose to pay you back. If so, you will receive interest in addition to the sum Ellie borrowed. Or, you may choose to leave your money in the business. Then, Ellie will share her profits with you. Either way, you use your money to make more money.

Investing in a business is not a sure thing. Ellie's flower shop might fail, and if it does, you could lose your money. But if the shop makes it big, you might make it big, too. Some investors make it _really_ big. Many people who invested in the computer company Microsoft when it was a struggling new company are millionaires today.

You can also invest in the **stock market**. By selling stock, companies can raise the large amounts of cash needed to do business. If the company makes a profit, it pays **dividends** to its stockholders based on the amount of stock each stockholder owns. The price of stock goes up and down depending on the success of the company and conditions in the stock market as a whole. Stockholders hope to buy stock when its price is low. Then, as the price goes up, they make money if they choose to sell.

Buying **bonds** is another kind of investment. When you buy a bond from the United States government or a business, you are loaning money. When you cash in the bonds, you will receive the face value plus a certain amount of interest. There are many types of bonds. Some are fairly safe investments, but others carry a risk of loss.

Quick Review 2: Why is an investment in a bank savings account safer than an investment in a business or in stocks?

_____

_____

_____

The Workforce

Unless you know where to find some buried treasure, chances are you're going to have a job someday. You might not have any idea what you want to do when you get out of school. On the other hand, you may already be dreaming of a certain career. Either way, it's a good idea to know something about the workforce and what kinds of opportunities are waiting for you as a member of it.

For almost 20 years now, the trend in American jobs has been away from manufacturing and toward service jobs. As manufacturing companies grow larger and do business all over the world, they often find it better to open factories in countries other than the United States. Workers often ask for less money in other countries; also, other costs of doing business are often lower. In addition, many industries need fewer workers because of improved **technology**—better, smarter equipment.

The **global economy** (goods and services produced by companies doing business all over the world) also has cut the number of agriculture and mining jobs in the United States. Much of the world's fruits, vegetables, and meat is produced outside the United States. Again, it is more profitable for global companies to buy them there and to sell them here. The same is true for raw materials used in industry.

Despite these changes, the American economy has produced millions of new jobs within the last 10 years. Service jobs in banking, investments, insurance, and real estate are growing. Even though manufacturing jobs have moved away, the money that runs these giant companies still comes from the

United States. The growth of computer technology has created many new jobs for people who can build and maintain computer systems and networks.

Although some high-wage jobs have been created, many more of the new jobs are low-wage jobs. It often seems as if fast-food restaurants and strip malls are springing up on every corner. Jobs in these new businesses usually do not pay a great deal of money, and opportunities to "move up" into more responsible positions are few.

Quick Review 3: What has caused changes in the job market in the last few years?

_____

_____

_____

_____

The Future

The employment picture will probably not change soon. Manufacturing jobs will remain hard to get; service jobs will be easier to get but may not pay very well. The computer boom will cause a high demand for people who can fix them when they break, as well as for people who can find new ways to make them useful in the workplace. There also is a great demand for teachers right now.

As the "baby boom" generation (people born between 1946 and 1964) gets older and leaves the workforce, there will be greater opportunities for young workers. The baby boomers will begin to retire early in the 21st century, which means the employment picture might start to change between 2005 and 2010. Because technology will keep moving forward at a speedy pace, however, it's hard to tell what that change might look like.

One thing is clear, however: If you stay in school, you have a much greater chance at a well-paying job than you'll have if you leave school. It's true of both genders and all races.

Yearly Earnings and Education, 1995

Gender or Race	Average Yearly Earnings for Non-High School Graduates	Average Yearly Earnings for High School Graduates
Male	$16,748	$26,333
Female	$ 9,790	$15,970
White	$14,234	$22,154
Black	$12,956	$17,072
Hispanic	$13,068	$18,333
All genders and races	$14,013	$21,431

The yearly earnings of people who go to college are even higher. The reason you hear so much about staying in school is that it really pays off.

Going Global

The global economy has changed buying, selling, and working for people everywhere. The rules are different now from what they were as little as 20 years ago. But why has the economy gone global?

Improved communication has made the world smaller. Money and information can travel from continent to continent in hours rather than days or weeks. Improved transportation makes it possible for products to be manufactured in a place far away from where the products are used. In short, the world is a smaller place today, thanks to technology.

In the global economy, businesses can pick and choose from a worldwide menu of raw materials, labor forces, and markets. For example, a restaurant chain can buy beef from Australia, potatoes from Idaho, and paper products from somewhere in Asia to supply its restaurants in South America. It doesn't do it because there are no beef producers, potato growers, or paper manufacturers in South America; the chain does it because it can get the best prices for the supplies it needs by "shopping" in the global marketplace.

The global economy rewards large international companies. It takes a lot of economic muscle to compete on a worldwide scale. Yet globalization also offers opportunity: Companies located anywhere have a chance to succeed almost everywhere. Or at least that's the theory.

One of the criticisms of the global economy is that capital—the money that makes the global economy run—is concentrated in the United States, Western Europe, and Japan. The labor force, meanwhile, is mostly found in the poorer countries of South America, Asia, and Africa. Companies "shop" for labor in these areas because it's less expensive. Because there is a large supply of workers in these countries, the price of labor is lower. Workers will take less money to do the jobs. A worker at a clothing factory in Vietnam, for example, could never hope to buy the clothes he or she makes for a wage of only a few cents an hour. And in fact, the clothing company may have no intention of selling its product in Vietnam. It's more likely that the clothing will be shipped to the United States or Europe for sale.

Quick Review 4: Name some other businesses or industries that are heavily involved in the global economy by buying, selling, or producing products in a number of countries.

_____

_____

_____

_____

_____

A Shoe Story

At one time, the northeastern United States was home to several major shoe producers. As time passed, these manufacturers were unable to compete with foreign producers, which made shoes that cost less. Factories closed. The American shoe industry is much smaller today than it was in years past.

The fate of the American shoe industry is an example of how the economic activities of a company based on another continent can have an effect on citizens of even a small American town. Those activities can affect the price people pay for shoes (and countless other items, big and small). They can also affect the futures of American citizens: for example, a person who may have hoped to work in a shoe factory until he or she reached retirement age.

We're All in This Together

In the global economy, the world's countries are linked. For example, countries all around the world struggle with the problem of **excess workers**. The combined forces of globalization and technology mean that many industries need fewer workers. People possessing certain skills find little or no demand for them in the labor market. A country such as the United States, which has traditionally paid its manufacturing workers high wages, sees high-wage jobs drain away to Mexico, South America, or other areas in which companies can get the same work done with less-expensive labor. Although American manufacturing workers are willing and able to work, they find it harder to compete in a global marketplace.

The business cycle also links countries with one another. In 1998, for example, Japan, Indonesia, and other Asian nations saw their powerful economies weaken. On the other side of the world, Americans wondered whether this so-called "Asian flu" was contagious. Could the long period of economic growth that began in 1993 be near an end? In the global economy, no country is completely isolated from the others.

The global economy presents workers, consumers, businesses, and governments with challenges unlike any faced in human history. When multinational corporations have bigger "economies" than many countries, what is the role of government supposed to be? Can governments still protect their citizens, their industries, and their environments? Although global trade is a benefit to businesses and consumers in many ways, what will become of the people who lose their jobs and their purchasing power because of it? In a world so closely interconnected, is there any way out of a worldwide financial meltdown, should one occur? World leaders of the 21st century must deal with these issues and others that have yet to appear.

What Do You Think?

Directions: Answer the questions on the lines provided. Be prepared to discuss your answers in class.

1. Name some other examples of contracts with which you are familiar. Why are those contracts needed?

_____

_____

_____

_____

_____

_____

_____

2. Look back at the earnings and education table on page 146. Do you see any workforce problems in the table? Describe them.

_____

_____

_____

_____

_____

_____

_____

_____

_____

Test Your Knowledge

Directions: Write a brief definition for each of the following:

1. Guarantee

_____

_____

_____

_____

_____

_____

2. Credit rating

_____

_____

_____

_____

_____

_____

3. Investment

_____

_____

_____

_____

_____

Directions: Read the passage below and use it to answer the questions that follow.

The country of Spasvania, located on an island, has beautiful mountains sloping down to its Pacific Ocean beaches. The beaches are great for swimming and fishing, and two rare species of tiger live in the mountains. Spasvanians believe the mountains may have deposits of several metals that can be used in industry, although the country has no large factories.

Spasvania has a population of 200,000. Most of the people live in Spasvania City, the country's capital. Many of them cannot find jobs. The country has a few banana plantations and some small factories that make decorations out of coconut shells. There also are a couple of resorts for tourists to visit.

Throughout its long history, Spasvania has kept to itself. Now, the country's president wants to bring the country into the global economy. Because you are an American expert on the global economy, the president has asked you for some advice.

4. What does Spasvania have to offer to the rest of the world?

   _____

   _____

5. What does the global economy offer to Spasvania?

   _____

   _____

6. Give two reasons why Spasvania should get into the global economy.

   _____

   _____

   _____

7. What choices will Spasvania have to make in deciding whether to enter the global economy?

   _____

   _____

Unit 3 Review Test

1. In a world of pure competition, which of the following is true?

   A. Some producers have a monopoly.

   B. Government regulates the activities of business.

   C. Supply and demand is the only factor affecting prices.

   D. Consumers do not have perfect information on goods and services to buy.

2. Which economic indicator shows changes in the cost of living?

   A. money supply

   B. Gross Domestic Product

   C. Consumer Price Index

   D. federal budget deficit

3. Carlos runs a stereo shop. Right now, he's unloading a truck full of speakers he plans to put on sale. From the point of view of the store, the speakers are

   A. microeconomic goods.

   B. investment goods.

   C. consumption goods.

   D. inventory goods.

4. The economy has three basic sectors: households, businesses, and

   A. banks.

   B. government.

   C. incentives.

   D. capital goods.

Directions: Look at the table, then use it to answer Number 5.

Gross Domestic Product Per Person, 1996

Country	Less than $1,000	$1,000 to $3,000	$3,000 to $10,000	$10,000 to $15,000	$15,000 or more
Azerbaijan		✓			
Botswana			✓		
Iceland					✓
Slovenia				✓	
Tuvalu	✓				

Source: *Information Please Almanac*

5. Which statement is true?

   A. The people of Tuvalu are, on the average, fairly rich.

   B. Slovenia has the largest population of any country shown in the table.

   C. Botswana's economy was larger in 1996 than in earlier years.

   D. Iceland is the most prosperous country shown in the table.

Talking with Karl and Adam

6. If you were to ask Karl Marx, he would most likely say that the value of anything comes from
   A. the price for which it can be sold.
   B. the labor of the workers who make it.
   C. the amount of capital it takes to make it.
   D. whatever people agree its value should be.

7. Which of these statements would Adam Smith most agree with?
   A. People should be free to make their own economic decisions.
   B. All of history is about struggles between economic classes.
   C. The management of colonies is a job for the government.
   D. Government has the right to limit working hours and wages.

8. The economies of Japan, Western Europe, and the United States are all examples of
   A. regulated capitalism.
   B. privatized socialism.
   C. capitalistic communism.
   D. nationalist mercantilism.

9. Some Americans argue that the government should cut spending on welfare and other government social programs. A possible effect of such decreases in government spending could be
   A. lower taxes.
   B. lower wages.
   C. higher deficits.
   D. larger government.

10. Which economic system has been spreading to new countries since the late 1980s?
    A. feudalism
    B. capitalism
    C. communism
    D. mercantilism

11. The company that made your computer says that if the computer breaks down within one year of the time you buy it, the company will fix it for free. This is an example of a

    A. credit rating.

    B. contract.

    C. dividend.

    D. warranty.

12. Which of the following statements about the American economy is true?

    A. Thousands of new manufacturing jobs have been created in the last 10 years.

    B. A high-school or college education has little impact on the earnings of workers.

    C. The American economy provides much of the capital for the global economy.

    D. The American economy is large enough to avoid problems that affect other world economies.

13. Although the stock market can be a risky investment, millions of Americans keep buying stocks. What is one reason why?

    A. People should ignore risk when using their own money.

    B. People believe the possible rewards are greater than the risks.

    C. Investing in the stock market is still safer than putting money in a bank.

    D. The stock market is the only way for an investor to help a business grow.

14. Which of the following inventions has most speeded the growth of the global economy within the last 10 years?

    A. more air travel

    B. refrigerated boxcars

    C. information technology

    D. factories powered by electricity

IN THIS UNIT

- Historic Documents
- The Constitution and the Bill of Rights
- Political Principles
- How Government Works

Left: *The ancient Greeks built beautiful temples and public buildings. Most are in ruins today, but another Greek invention—democracy—is going strong around the world.*

Civics

Government is the way societies do things that individuals cannot do by themselves. Think about it—how many of us could build a street, run a fire department, or track down a criminal? Instead, we give our governments the power to do these jobs for us. The power is ours. Government is how we use it.

Before the founding of the United States, no country had ever given its people as much power as the Founding Fathers gave us. That's why the United States is sometimes called "a great experiment in self-government." By calling it an "experiment," we remind ourselves that it's not finished yet; it still might fail. It's up to each new generation of Americans to see that it doesn't.

Lesson 16

Historic Documents

© 1999 Buckle Down Publishing Company. DO NOT DUPLICATE.

IT'S IMPORTANT:

■ The Declaration of Independence is the basic statement of what Americans believe about the rights of people and the reason for government.

■ The Declaration also explains why the colonies were breaking away from Great Britain.

John Adams got the celebration part right. For more than 200 years, Americans have held parades, shot off fireworks, played games, and enjoyed many other ways of celebrating the nation's birthday. The only part Adams got wrong was the date. The Continental Congress voted for independence on July 2, 1776, but the Declaration of Independence was signed two days later.

There is much more to the Declaration of Independence than an excuse to light sparklers and have picnics. The ideas contained in the Declaration are the words upon which the United States of America was founded. Every American should know what those ideas are and what they mean.

> *July 2 ought to be [remembered] . . . with Pomp and Parade, with Shows, Games, Sports, Guns, Bells, Bonfires, and Illuminations from one End of this Continent to the other . . . .*
>
> —**John Adams**, 1776

Before the Declaration

Thomas Jefferson wrote most of the Declaration of Independence, but he didn't make it up all by himself. He based it on many ideas from English history, including some earlier documents.

In 1215, English barons, or noble landowners, met with King John and forced him to sign the **Magna Carta**. This document was important in developing constitutional law in England. The barons demanded that the king uphold the law. The Magna Carta said that the king could not tax the barons without the approval of Parliament. Barons were permitted to have trials by jury when accused of committing crimes. Although ordinary citizens were not mentioned, the Magna Carta provided an important first step toward representative democracy.

In 1688, the English Parliament forced England's Catholic king, James II, from the throne. Parliament invited James's daughter and her husband to be the new rulers of England. In 1689, **William and Mary** signed the **English Bill of Rights**, which made Parliament stronger than any king or queen. Rulers could no longer change laws on their own. They could not raise taxes or cancel elections without Parliament's approval. The Bill of Rights also protected rights of individuals, guaranteed trial by jury, and outlawed cruel and unusual punishments.

In 1620, the Pilgrims reached the coast of Cape Cod, Massachusetts. Before leaving the Mayflower, they met to sign the **Mayflower Compact**. The 41 signers agreed to work together to write "just and equall Lawes" for "ye generall good of ye colonie." It was the first agreement for self-government in the New World.

Quick Review 1: Briefly explain the importance of each of the following:

Magna Carta: _____

_____

_____

English Bill of Rights: _____

_____

_____

What Does the Declaration Mean?

Although Thomas Jefferson's language can be hard to understand, his ideas are very clear. He began by saying that it was necessary for the colonies to "dissolve the political bands" that held them to Great Britain and that the colonies wanted the world to know why this was true. Then came the most famous part of the Declaration of Independence. It is reprinted here, along with an explanation of what the language means.

We hold these truths to be self-evident:	We believe that the following is very clear:
That all men are created equal;	That no person is better than any other person;
That they are endowed by their Creator with certain unalienable rights;	That each person is born with rights that cannot be changed or taken away by anyone;
That among these are life, liberty, and the pursuit of happiness.	These rights include life; the freedom to act or believe as you choose; and the freedom to do those things that you believe will lead to your happiness.
To secure these rights, governments are instituted among men,	To protect these rights, people form governments.
Deriving their powers from the consent of the governed.	Governments get only the amount of power that the people want to give them.

This part of the Declaration of Independence is still the basic statement of what Americans believe about people and their governments.

Quick Review 2: According to the Declaration of Independence, what three rights are people born with?

_____

_____

_____

_____

Why do people form governments? _____

_____

_____

Who decides how much power a government will receive?

_____

_____

_____

_____

Why Did They Do It?

The Declaration of Independence was written to explain why the colonies were breaking away from Great Britain. After Jefferson had explained why people form governments, he made it clear why the breakup had to happen.

Whenever any form of government becomes destructive of these ends,	Whenever a government harms the rights of the people,
It is the right of the people to alter or abolish it,	The people have the right to change their government or get rid of it completely,
And to institute new government,	And to form a new government.
Laying its foundation on such principles as shall seem most likely to effect their safety and happiness.	The people can set up the new government in any way, as long as they believe it will lead to their safety and happiness.

What Else Does It Say?

Much of the rest of the Declaration of Independence is a list of the many ways in which the government of King George III had become "destructive of" the rights of the colonists. He had refused to allow them to have representative government and fair courts; he had taxed them illegally; he had sent soldiers to attack and kill them; he had refused to listen when they asked for his help.

The Declaration of Independence ends by saying that the colonies had the right to be independent from Great Britain, and they were declaring themselves to be free. It was signed by 53 representatives, including John Hancock, John Adams, Samuel Adams, Benjamin Franklin, and Thomas Jefferson. "In support of this Declaration," they wrote, "we pledge to each other our lives, our fortunes, and our sacred honor."

In short, the signers of the Declaration believed that Britain was not living up to its responsibilities. Governments are supposed to protect the natural rights people are born with. If governments do not, they should be changed so that they will. The signers were willing to give their lives to make a country based on these ideas. So were many other Americans.

Today's Americans still believe in the ideas expressed in the Declaration of Independence. Other people in other countries have adopted these ideas also.

The signers of the Declaration of Independence were taking a dangerous step. If the Revolution failed, they would face prison and death for being rebels.

John Hancock, president of the Continental Congress, was the first to sign. His signature is larger than all the others. Hancock said he wanted to make sure King George III could read it without his glasses. Historians believe Hancock was the only one to sign on July 4. The other signers added their names over the next several weeks.

What Do You Think?

Directions: Answer the questions on the lines provided. Be prepared to discuss your answers in class.

1. Explain some ways that the government protects our rights to life, liberty, and the pursuit of happiness.

   _____

   _____

   _____

   _____

2. Read the following statement:

The Declaration of Independence says we are born with the right to the pursuit of happiness, but we also have laws that keep us from doing certain things. That's not right. We should be able to do whatever we want, as long as it makes us happy.

Do you agree or disagree with the statement? Give reasons for your answer.

_____

_____

_____

_____

_____

Test Your Knowledge

Directions: Fill in the blanks in each statement.

1. The Declaration of Independence was written by Thomas _____.

2. "We hold these truths to be self-evident; that all men are _____

_____."

3. "Among these [unalienable rights] are _____,

_____, and the

_____."

4. "To secure these rights, _____ are instituted among men."

5. "Whenever a government becomes destructive of these rights, it is the right of

_____ to alter or abolish it."

In 1787, it was clear that the United States was in trouble. The **Articles of Confederation**, a plan of government going back to the Revolutionary War, wasn't working. The Articles made state governments stronger than the national government. As a result, the national government was weak, and the country was almost out of money. Meanwhile, the states refused to work together. Instead, they wanted to fight with each other. When a group of farmers threatened to rebel against the government of Massachusetts, some American leaders decided a change was needed.

A convention was called to rewrite the Articles of Confederation. It ended up writing an entirely new plan for the government of the United States. The **Constitution** set up the basic framework of government still used today.

Divided Powers

The Constitution of the United States gives some powers to the **federal** (national) government and leaves others to the states, or to smaller governments, like counties and cities. Powers were not just handed out at random. There are very good reasons for the way it was done.

Imagine what it would be like if Virginia had its own money. When you went on a trip to Maryland, North Carolina, or any other state, you would have to change your Virginia money into the other state's money or your money would be no good. There was a similar problem before the Constitution was written. Each state had its own money, and the system was bad for business and difficult for ordinary people. The Constitution gives the power to print money and make coins to the federal government, not the states.

Imagine what it would be like if each state ran its own post office. We know that a first-class stamp costs the same amount of money in all 50 states. Think about this: What if the cost of a stamp was different in every state? How would you mail a letter or a package to Los Angeles if you needed a different stamp for every state your letter would go through? The Constitution gives the power to set up a post office to the federal government, not the states.

Printing money, delivering the mail, and other large tasks like declaring war and dealing with foreign countries, can be done best by the federal government. Other jobs can be done best by smaller governments. For example, the states and local communities have the power to set up school systems and to make laws about marriage and divorce. State laws cannot violate the Constitution, however.

Lesson 17
The Constitution and the Bill of Rights

IT'S IMPORTANT:

■ The Constitution replaced the Articles of Confederation.

■ The Constitution is the basic plan for American government.

■ The federal government is divided into three branches.

■ The federal government's power is also separated.

■ The Constitution can be amended.

■ The first 10 amendments, the Bill of Rights, guarantee personal freedom to all Americans.

Some powers belong to *both* the states and the federal government. Both can collect taxes and have court systems, for example.

Power was divided because many Americans feared a powerful federal government. They remembered how the powerful British government had treated them, and they didn't want it to happen again. The states were given as much power as possible without making the federal government too weak.

Quick Review 1: How does the Constitution keep the federal government from getting too powerful?

_____

_____

_____

Separation of Powers

The Constitution took the federal government's power and divided it even further. It created three branches of government to do the work. This is known as **separation of powers**.

Separation of powers is made stronger by a system of **checks and balances**. No branch of the government can do its job alone. Each one needs the other two.

- Congress cannot make laws without the president's approval. Any bill passed by Congress must be signed by the president. If he or she does not approve of the bill, he or she can **veto** it, and it will not become law. If Congress strongly approves of a law, the president's wishes are not the last word. Congress can take a vote to **override** the veto. If the override is passed, the bill becomes a law.

- Because it's very hard to write laws that will cover anything that might happen, the courts have to apply the law to different situations. Sometimes this means that courts decide that a law means something different from what Congress and the president think it means.

- Courts can even throw out laws they believe are against the Constitution. If a law is thrown out, Congress and the president have the right to make a new law to replace it. Although this power is an

The Preamble

The first words of the Constitution, known as the **Preamble**, describe the goals of the people who wrote it:

"We the people of the United States, in order to form a more perfect Union, establish justice, insure domestic tranquility, provide for the common defense, promote the general welfare, and to secure the blessings of liberty to ourselves and our posterity, do ordain and establish this Constitution for the United States of America."

In short, the Constitution was written to set up a government that would keep all Americans peaceful, safe, happy, and free, including Americans who would be born after it was written.

Branches of Government

The **executive branch** is the president. This branch sees that the laws made by the legislative branch are carried out.

Congress is the **legislative branch**. It makes the laws.

The **judicial branch**, made up of the courts, is responsible for applying the laws.

important part of checks and balances, it is not in the Constitution. You'll learn where it came from in Lesson 19.

FAST FACT

Another way for a president to check the federal courts is to appoint judges who share his or her beliefs. Congress must approve all federal judges. Much of the time, they do, but not always. In 1988, President Ronald Reagan appointed Robert Bork to the Supreme Court. The United States Senate did not agree with some of Bork's beliefs and refused to approve him. Reagan was forced to appoint a different judge to the court.

Quick Review 2: How does the system of checks and balances keep one branch of government from getting more powerful than the other two?

_____

_____

_____

_____

_____

Congress and the President

Under the Articles of Confederation, there was one house of Congress and no president. The Constitution changed this.

The largest states wanted Congress to be based on population. In other words, the more people a state had, the more representatives it would have in Congress. The smallest states wanted a Congress in which each state had the same number of votes. The convention nearly fell apart in the fight over this issue. In the end, the delegates agreed to have two houses of Congress, a House of Representatives based on population, and a Senate with an equal number of votes for each state.

To keep them close to the people, House members would be elected every two years. Any bill having to do with spending tax money was required to come from the House. Senate members would not be elected by the people at all. They were to be chosen by the state legislatures.

Some delegates did not want a president. They felt that putting power into the hands of one person would make that person a king. Others disagreed, saying that somebody had to be responsible for carrying out the laws. The delegates settled on an elected president, chosen every four years. The president would not be chosen directly by voters, but by an electoral college. Members of the electoral college were to be chosen by state legislatures. This was done to keep the people from making a bad choice for president.

A Living Document

The Constitution explained what Congress was and what it would do. It set up the office of the president and explained its powers. It created a court system for the new country. It divided the powers of government between these branches of government and between the federal government and the states. It made laws for the relationships between the states.

The delegates also wanted to make the Constitution a document that could grow and change with the country, so they allowed it to be amended, or changed. If Congress and the president agreed on a proposed **amendment**, it would be sent to the states to be voted on. When two-thirds of the state legislatures voted in favor of the amendment, it would be added to the Constitution. Hundreds of amendments have been proposed in the years since the Constitution was written, yet only 27 have been added. Some of these were changes to the original Constitution; others were additions.

The Constitution was signed on September 17, 1787. It was sent to each state legislature to be approved. Americans everywhere argued over the Constitution. Some said it would make the federal government too strong. Others thought it was the only way to save the United States. Those who favored the Constitution put their arguments into newspaper articles known today as *The Federalist Papers*. By June of 1788, nine of the 13 states had ratified (approved) the Constitution, putting it into effect.

The Bill of Rights

A few delegates wouldn't sign the Constitution. They said it did not go far enough in protecting the rights of citizens. Many of those opposed to ratifying it shared this belief. They insisted that the Constitution needed a Bill of Rights to make Americans truly free. In 1791, Congress approved 10 amendments to the Constitution, making up the **Bill of Rights**.

Congress borrowed from two important Virginia documents in writing the Bill of Rights: the **Declaration of Rights**, adopted less than a month before the Declaration of Independence and the **Virginia Statute for Religious Freedom**, written by Thomas Jefferson in 1786.

- The First Amendment protects freedom of speech, the press, and religion. (The British government and Church of England were closely tied. The Virginia Statute declared that government and religion should be separate; the Bill of Rights adopted the Virginia idea.)

- The Second Amendment protects the right of citizens to keep guns for defending themselves.

- The Third Amendment forbids the government from requiring citizens to let soldiers live in their homes, as the British did before the Revolution.

- The Fourth Amendment keeps the homes of citizens safe from unlawful search. The government cannot search without permission from a court.

- The Fifth Amendment protects citizens from having to testify against themselves in court. It makes sure the law will run its course before the life, liberty, or property of any citizen can be taken away.

- The Sixth Amendment contains the right to a trial by jury if a person is accused of a crime. It also makes sure that citizens will be able to face the people who accuse them of a crime.

A Look Ahead

How will the Constitution and laws change in the new century just ahead?

In recent years, the Constitution has been used to correct wrongs in society. Women, African Americans, and other groups have faced **discrimination** (unfair treatment) because of gender or race. **Affirmative action** programs give these groups jobs or education to make up for unfair treatment in the past. Today, some Americans wonder if these laws are right. Courts in some states have already ended affirmative action programs, saying that they are unfair to people not covered by them.

Courts have already answered a few questions about computers and the Internet, but there will be more. For example, the Fourth Amendment does not allow unreasonable searches. If the government looks at your e-mail without permission from a judge, is that an "unreasonable search"? As more and more of us use e-mail and the Internet, the courts must decide how the Constitution and laws apply.

- The Seventh Amendment gives the right to a jury trial in **civil** (non-criminal) court cases.

- The Eighth Amendment forbids cruel punishments and heavy fines.

- Amendments Nine and Ten make sure that the rights of government are limited, while the rights of citizens are not.

What Do You Think?

Directions: Answer the questions on the lines provided. Be prepared to discuss your answers in class.

1. In 1787, why was it important for the United States to "form a more perfect Union"?

_____

_____

_____

_____

_____

_____

2. Give two examples of how the Bill of Rights affects your life.

_____

_____

_____

_____

_____

Test Your Knowledge

Directions: Write a short description of each document listed. Be sure to include its purpose and the year in which it was written.

1. Constitution:

   _____

   _____

   _____

2. Bill of Rights:

   _____

   _____

   _____

Directions: Match the phrases with the documents that they come from. Write the letter of the document next to the number of the phrase. The document letters will be used more than once.

B: Bill of Rights

C: Constitution

_____ 3. "No person . . . shall be deprived of life, liberty, or property without due process of law."

_____ 4. "All legislative powers shall be vested in a Congress of the United States, which shall consist of a Senate and House of Representatives."

_____ 5. "We the people of the United States, in order to form a more perfect Union, establish justice, insure domestic tranquillity. . . ."

_____ 6. "Congress shall make no law . . . prohibiting the free exercise [of religion] or abridging the freedom of speech or the press. . . ."

_____ 7. ". . . the accused shall enjoy the right to a speedy and public trial by a jury. . . ."

_____ 8. "The Congress shall have power . . . to declare war . . . to raise and support armies . . . to provide and maintain a navy."

Directions: Answer the question below on the lines provided.

9. What is the difference between the Constitution and the Bill of Rights?

_____

_____

_____

_____

_____

_____

Political Principles

Virginia has played an important role in the development of democracy in this country. It was the home to the first elected government in colonial America. It was also the birthplace of the writer of the Declaration of Independence, as well as four of the first five presidents of the United States. It might surprise you to learn, however, that the first government in Virginia was anything but democratic.

Jamestown and the Virginia Company Charters

In 1606, King James I of England granted a charter to the **Virginia Company of London**, allowing the company to create a colony in America. The investors in the Virginia Company were not concerned about creating a new, free society. Their main goal was profit. They hoped the colonists would find riches in the New World that could be brought back to England.

The charter of the Virginia company created two councils: one in England and one in the new colony of Jamestown. The council in England was mostly made up of members of the Virginia Company, appointed by the king. They created many rules that the colonists had to follow: everything from exactly where the colony would be founded to how often the colonists had to attend church.

Because the investors wanted to make money, the colonists were ordered to spend much of their time looking for gold. Because there was no gold to be found, this ended up wasting valuable time. The colonists could have used that time to plant crops, hunt for food, and build sturdy homes. As a result, the first year at Jamestown was a long, hungry, difficult one.

The ruling council in Jamestown did little to help. The 13-member council was appointed by company members in England. The colonists had no say as to who would lead them. The council members often fought with each other, and little was accomplished. After a few years, the Virginia Company decided that their colony needed a governor who would be in charge. This did not change the basic fact that the colonists still had no say in their government. The governor was appointed, not elected, and he had absolute authority over the colony.

By 1619, the Jamestown colony had begun to improve. Colonists discovered they could grow tobacco and sell it in England. This gave the settlement more stability. The ruling council in England decided to give the colonists more

IT'S IMPORTANT:

- The Virginia Company Charter organized the first government of the Jamestown colony.

- The House of Burgesses expanded the role of colonists in government.

- The Virginia Declaration of Rights and Virginia Statute for Religious Freedom expanded personal rights in Virginia.

- The Virginia Constitution organizes the government of the commonwealth.

freedom. The colonists were allowed to create an assembly that would help make laws for the settlement. This assembly became known as the **House of Burgesses**. It was the first elected government body in America, and it became a model for many of the other colonies.

Quick Review 1: List some of the problems the Virginia Company charter caused for the early colonists at Jamestown.

_____

_____

_____

The Virginia Declaration of Rights and the Virginia Statute for Religious Freedom

The House of Burgesses was the elected government of Virginia for over 150 years. As tensions grew between the American colonies and Britain, however, Virginians started to rethink the role of government. The governor of Virginia was still appointed by the king. If Virginians were going to break away from Britain, what kind of government would they put in place of the British king and Parliament?

Part of the answer came in the form of a document called the **Virginia Declaration of Rights** written by **George Mason** and adopted by the Virginia Convention of Delegates in June of 1776. The document spelled out the purpose of government, as Virginians saw it. The Virginia Declaration included several ideas that would be included in the Declaration of Independence and the Bill of Rights. These included the belief that government gets its power from the people and that the main purpose of government is to protect the rights of citizens. The Virginia Declaration also stated that there should be three separate branches of government: executive, legislative, and judicial.

The Virginia Declaration also listed several specific rights each citizen was entitled to. Among these were freedom of the press, freedom of religion, and the right to a trial by jury. All of these are guaranteed to each American today in the Bill of Rights.

Ten years later, in 1786, another important document came from the pen of a famous Virginian, Thomas Jefferson. The **Virginia Statute for Religious Freedom** made it illegal for the government to support one religion over another. The government was also forbidden to interfere with the religious beliefs or practices of individual citizens. This was a major change from the early days at Jamestown when colonists had to attend church twice a day or risk a fine or imprisonment. Jefferson's statute ended the favoritism Virginia's government had shown toward the Church of England and became a model for religious freedom throughout the newly formed United States.

Quick Review 2: List ways in which the government described in the Virginia Declaration of Rights and the Virginia Statute for Religious Freedom was different from the government set up by the Virginia Company charter.

_____

_____

_____

_____

The Virginia Constitution: Yesterday and Today

When Virginia became a state in 1776, its leaders wrote a state constitution. Since then, there have been five more state constitutions. The current state constitution took effect in 1971. Each constitution is at least slightly different than the one that came before, but all share many of the basic ideas taken from earlier documents you have read about in this lesson.

The Virginia constitution, like the Constitution of the United States, divides government into three branches and creates checks and balances to keep any one branch from becoming too powerful. The legislative branch, called the **General Assembly**, is the descendant of the House of Burgesses, created over 350 years ago in colonial Virginia.

This division of government is very similar to that proposed in the Virginia Declaration of Rights. In fact, a number of the important parts of the Virginia constitution closely resemble the Virginia Declaration of Rights and the Virginia Statute for Religious Freedom.

For example, the Virginia constitution declares that the people are the source of political power and that government exists for the benefit of all people. The constitution also calls for free elections so that "the consent of the governed" can be given to the government. The state constitution also states a number of rights that all citizens have, including freedom of speech, freedom to assemble, and the right to a jury trial. All of these ideas were originally part of the Virginia Declaration of Rights in 1776.

The Virginia constitution also guarantees freedom of religion and says that the state will not favor or support any particular church. This idea comes not only from the Virginia Declaration of Rights, but also from the Virginia Statute of Religious Freedom.

It is important to remember, however, that the current Virginia constitution differs from these earlier documents and from earlier versions of the state constitution in several ways. The first Virginia constitutions stated that the only people eligible to vote were white male landowners. Women, blacks (whether free or slave), and poor people did not have the right to vote when Virginia became a state. Today, anyone who legally lives in the state and is over 18 can vote in Virginia. Voters also have more direct say in who their leaders are. For example, the first Virginia constitution said that the governor of the state would be elected by the legislature, not by the people themselves. Today, the voters decide who will hold the highest office in the state. Virginia's government still requires "consent of the governed," but the thinking behind that phrase has been expanded greatly in the last two centuries.

Not only do more people have the right to vote today, but now people have more ways of participating in the process of government. People can write their representatives, send them e-mail, make donations to campaigns, or do volunteer work for their favorite candidates. People can learn about the issues through newspapers, magazines, television, radio, and the Internet. Now more than ever, it is possible for people to give their informed consent to the government.

Quick Review 3: Name two ways today's Virginians can participate in government that were not available in 1776.

_____

_____

_____

Political Principles of Virginia's Historic Documents

Document	Source of Political Power	Role of Government	View of Individual	Overall Philosophy
Virginia Company Charters	The king	To maintain discipline and order through control	A sort of "employee" whose job it is to help the company succeed	Individuals must be controlled in order to create a stable community
Virginia Declaration of Rights	The people	To protect the rights of the individual	Every person holds certain rights that cannot be taken away	Government should obey the will of the majority while protecting the rights of the individual
Virginia Statute for Religious Freedom	The people	To avoid interference with personal beliefs	Each person is a freethinking being who is entitled to his or her beliefs	Individual freedom of belief is more important than creating a community that shares the same beliefs
Virginia Constitution	The people	To limit itself so that liberties can be protected and exercised	Each citizen is a member of society who has both rights and responsibilities in a democracy	Democratic government is the best way of securing the rights of the individual

What Do You Think?

Directions: Answer the question on the lines provided. Be prepared to discuss your answer in class.

The Virginia Company of London gave the Jamestown colonists more freedom—including the right to create an elected assembly—after tobacco became an important cash crop. Why do you think this happened? Why might the beginning of tobacco farming cause political changes in the colony?

_____

_____

_____

_____

_____

_____

Test Your Knowledge

Directions: Match the statement with the document it describes. Some documents will be used more than once.

_____ 1. Written by Thomas Jefferson

_____ 2. Signed by King James I of England

_____ 3. Has been changed five times since it was first written

_____ 4. Helped inspire the Bill of Rights in the U.S. Constitution

_____ 5. Ended Virginia's official connection to the Church of England

_____ 6. Written by George Mason

_____ 7. Established the colony of Jamestown

_____ 8. Was the last of the four documents to be written

   A. Virginia Company Charters
   B. Virginia Constitution
   C. Virginia Declaration of Rights
   D. Virginia Statute for Religious Freedom

Directions: Next to each event, write the year in which it happened.

_____ 9. The Virginia Declaration of Rights written

_____ 10. Charter granted to the Virginia Company of London

_____ 11. Virginia Statute of Religious Freedom enacted

_____ 12. House of Burgesses created

Directions: Briefly define and describe the importance of the following terms.

13. House of Burgesses:

_____

_____

_____

_____

14. "Consent of the governed":

_____

_____

_____

_____

Lesson  19

How Government Works

In the American system of government, the federal (national) government and the states divide the power of government. The Constitution of the United States also divides the federal government's power into three branches: legislative, executive, and judicial. This division is called separation of powers. The system was designed to keep any one part of the government from becoming more powerful than the others.

Each branch has its own job to perform. The Constitution carefully divides the powers of each one:

- The legislative branch (House of Representatives and Senate) makes laws;

- The executive branch (President and executive agencies) carries out laws; and

- The judicial branch (courts) interprets laws.

Along with the separation of powers, the Constitution includes a system of checks and balances. To keep any branch from becoming too powerful, each branch checks, or holds back, the power of the others. For example, the president can check Congress by vetoing laws; Congress can check the president by overriding the veto; the Supreme Court can check both the president and Congress by declaring laws unconstitutional (against the Constitution). Like separation of powers, the system of checks and balances is designed to ensure that the power of each branch is balanced by the power of the others.

Quick Review 1: What's the difference between separation of powers and checks and balances?

_____

_____

_____

_____

_____

_____

_____

Functions of the Federal Government

Some (not all) of the activities of the federal government are shown here.

The Legislative Branch (Congress):	**The Executive Branch (president and executive agencies):**	**The Judicial Branch (Supreme Court or federal courts):**
• writes proposed legislation • holds committee hearings • overrides a presidential veto • confirms executive appointments made by the president • impeaches or removes judges or the president • proposes and passes Constitutional amendments before ratification by the states • declares war	• proposes legislation • vetoes legislation • calls special legislative sessions • appoints federal judges • recommends appointments to certain jobs in government • coordinates work of agencies (such as the FBI, the Social Security Administration, or Cabinet departments) • enforces treaties and federal laws • commands the armed forces	• declares legislation or executive actions unconstitutional • conducts trials • sentences convicted persons

Quick Review 2: Write the name of the branch that was responsible for each action listed below.

Passed Americans With Disabilities Act, 1992: _____

Appointed Janet Reno, first woman to be U.S. attorney general, 1993: _____

_____

Approved Janet Reno's appointment: _____

Decided that legal restrictions on Internet content violated the First Amendment, 1997:

_____

Impeached President Clinton, 1998: _____

Branches at Work

In a system of checks and balances, the roles of the three branches are closely related. We say that the legislative branch makes laws, but the lawmaking process is not quite that simple.

New laws are proposed as **bills**. These are introduced by members of the legislature to be studied and voted upon by the whole legislature. Yet the individual legislators are not the only people who can come up with ideas for bills. Presidents and governors have their own ideas for bills. They can't introduce bills on their own, but they can create them for a friendly member of the legislature to introduce. Sometimes, groups or individuals may want a bill to be considered by the legislature. Again, those groups can write bills, but it's up to a member of the legislature to introduce them. At that point, the bills go through the process of study, hearings, and voting like any other bill.

Legislative bodies don't have time to decide every question about every subject. When Congress passes a law about food safety, for example, it does not take time to hear and vote on every detail of how food will be kept safe. Instead, it is more likely to do something like this: It gives the authority for overseeing food safety to the Food and Drug Administration (FDA), a government **agency**. Then, Congress gives the FDA the power to make any rules needed to ensure food safety. The rules have the force of law, even though each rule is not voted on by Congress.

Government agencies such as the FDA are usually part of the executive branch. This branch of government is overseen by the governor or president, as part of the executive's responsibility to carry out the laws. Such agencies have a major impact because of the power they are given by Congress or the state legislature. They are sometimes criticized for making rules that don't match what some members of Congress want. Yet in a society as complicated as ours, it would be very difficult to get along without powerful agencies to put laws to work.

The Judicial Branch

The Constitution provided for a court system, but left the details to be worked out by Congress. The courts themselves have also defined their roles. For example, the Supreme Court and other federal courts can declare laws unconstitutional and throw them out. This power is not in the Constitution. It has existed since 1803. In the case of *Marbury v. Madison*, Supreme Court justice John Marshall overturned a federal law, claiming that the law violated the Constitution. Ever since, the Supreme Court has had the power to declare laws unconstitutional.

The power of **judicial review** gives the federal courts an equal share of power with the legislative and executive branches of the federal government. Most states permit their highest courts to review state laws to make sure they do not violate the state constitution.

Court systems can be very complicated, and they vary from state to state. There are two basic types of court cases: **criminal** cases and **civil** cases. In criminal cases, a person is (or persons are) accused of breaking a law. The courts must determine if a law has been broken and if so, what the punishment should be. Civil cases involve disputes among persons or groups of people. Courts must determine which person or group has the law on their side. Often, the losing side in a civil case must pay **damages** to the winning side.

Although the systems vary from state to state, each state has a system for **appeals** of criminal and civil cases. (So does the federal court system.) State and federal laws state where most cases will be heard first. A convicted person or the loser of a civil case can take their case to a **court of appeals**, where they may argue that the outcome of their original case was incorrect. Sometimes courts of appeals overturn decisions that come to them from lower courts. They may find that the judge or jury made mistakes or that the rights of an accused person were violated.

At the state and federal level, there is often more than one level of appeals court. The highest court is the Supreme Court, which is sometimes called the "court of last resort." If the federal Supreme Court chooses to rule on a case (and it doesn't have to), its word is final.

Quick Review 3: Where does the concept of judicial review come from?

_____

_____

_____

State Government

State governments put federalism into practice. The Virginia constitution set up the state's government in 1776.

The state government of Virginia is structured as follows:

- Legislative branch: the **General Assembly**, which has two houses. The **Senate** has 40 members; the **House of Delegates** has 100. Senators serve four-year terms and delegates serve two-year terms. The General Assembly makes the laws for the state. Like the federal legislative branch, bills must be introduced by a member of the legislature.

- Executive branch: the **governor** and executive agencies responsible for running state offices. Voters elect the governor, lieutenant governor, and the attorney general. The governor then appoints the secretary of the commonwealth, adjutant general, treasurer, and comptroller. The legislature elects the state auditor.

- Judicial branch: state courts. The **Supreme Court of Virginia** has seven members. The **Court of Appeals of Virginia** hears cases that have already been decided by lower courts to decide whether they were handled correctly. Below the Court of Appeals of Virginia are the **circuit courts**. There are 122 circuit courts in Virginia. These courts hear both civil and criminal trials. They are the only courts in which juries decide the verdict. The **district courts** hear less serious civil and criminal trials; there, judges decide the verdicts. There are several types of lower courts that hear cases of particular kinds, such as **juvenile** and **domestic relations**.

  All judges in Virginia are elected by the General Assembly and serve terms from 6 years (for the lowest courts) to 12 years (for the Supreme Court of Virginia).

The legislative, executive, and judicial branches of the Virginia state government have many of the same types of power held by the federal legislative, executive, and judicial branches. For example, the General Assembly passes state laws. The governor can sign or veto laws and make appointments to state offices. The courts examine state laws to make sure they do not violate the state constitution, and they hold trials and pass sentences.

Local Government

Local governments have a relationship to the state that is similar to the relationship the state has with the federal government. Some activities of government are best done on the local level because local governments are closer to the people of their areas than the state government.

Local governments in Virginia include counties, independent cities, and towns. Virginia has 95 counties. Voters in each county elect a **board of supervisors** to run the county government (except Arlington, which has a **county board**). Voters in most counties also elect other officials, such as the sheriff, the county treasurer, and the county clerk.

Virginia has more than 41 **independent cities**. To qualify as an independent city, a town must have at least 5,000 people. The local governments of these cities are independent of the county government. All of these cities are run by a **council-manager** government. Some smaller towns also have council-manager governments, while others have **mayor-council** governments.

Quick Review 4: List some state officials who are chosen by each group.

Voters: _____

_____

General Assembly:_____

_____

Governor: _____

_____

Towns in Virginia have one of two types of government. What are the two forms?

_____

_____

Parties and Elections

Americans elect thousands of people to office each year. Most candidates run as members of a **political party**.

Today, Americans define a political party as an organization of citizens working together to achieve common political goals. Political parties have two basic functions that allow them to achieve their goals:

- They **nominate** (select) candidates for public office.

- They develop a **platform**, or official positions, on issues facing society.

The United States has had two major political parties throughout most of its history. The party system began with the Federalists and the Anti-Federalists, who disagreed over whether the Constitution should be ratified. Other major parties in American history have included the Whigs, Know-Nothings, Populists, and Progressives. The major parties are now the **Republicans** and the **Democrats**. There are many other smaller parties.

More than 200 years ago, George Washington warned Americans that political parties would be bad for the country. Yet even before he left office, parties were becoming a fact of life in American politics. Many Americans today agree with Washington. They argue that the two major parties are more interested in getting and keeping power than they are in solving the problems facing society. Voters would be wiser if they chose candidates based on what they stand for instead of what party they belong to.

Other Americans believe that in a democracy as large and diverse as the United States, political parties are necessary. They argue that without party labels, it would be too difficult for voters to decide between candidates. Most voters have a sense of what the major parties stand for, and it helps them make choices on election day.

Quick Review 5: What three purposes do political parties serve in the United States today?

_____

_____

_____

_____

Running for the Nomination

To run for some local offices, the only requirements are to fill out an application and get enough signatures of voters on a nominating petition. It may not even be necessary for you to declare a party. Just fill out the paperwork correctly and your name will be listed on the ballot when election day comes.

The process is more complicated for other local and state level offices, as well as in national politics. The major parties officially nominate one candidate for each office. What happens if, for example, seven Democrats all want the party nomination for the same office? In the United States, parties select nominees in two ways: **primary elections** and **conventions**.

In a primary election, all certified candidates for the party's nomination appear on the party's ballot. Certified candidates are required to get voter signatures on a nominating petition, and they may have to follow other rules set by the party. Next, voters choose the candidates they prefer. In most primary states, the candidate with the most votes wins the nomination.

At one time, political parties selected their candidates for all elected offices through conventions, which are meetings of party members. These conventions were sometimes criticized for not including enough party members in the decision-making process. Primary elections were created about 100 years ago to open up the nominating process. Parties still hold regular conventions at the local and state levels. These conventions develop party platforms and either nominate candidates for office or approve the results of primary elections.

Every four years, the Republican and Democratic parties hold national conventions. Officially, the national conventions meet to nominate candidates for president and vice president, although the presidential nominee is usually determined in advance through primaries and conventions in each state. The national conventions also develop national platforms.

After all the primaries and conventions are over, the candidates nominated by each party face each other in the general election.

The Campaign

Many political campaigns take place each year for local, state, or federal offices. The candidates or their parties try to win votes through TV and radio advertising, mailings, personal appearances, and other appeals for support.

Advertising is a big part of major campaigns for president, governor, and seats in Congress. Candidates advertise themselves like any other advertised product. Such advertising should be evaluated carefully, like advertising for any other product. Is it truthful? Will the product do what it promises? Because advertising is expensive, money is an important factor in many campaigns. People who have it or can get it stand a better chance of winning than people who have less money to work with.

Although most major campaigns are heavily influenced by advertising, a smart voter will not depend on advertising alone. Newspapers, magazines, and Internet sites are good sources for large amounts of information about candidates. A well-informed voter is better able to make an intelligent choice on election day.

Above: *Texas Senator Phil Gramm faces reporters while campaigning for the 1996 Republican presidential nomination in Des Moines, Iowa. Photo by David Peterson, copyright © 1996, the Des Moines Register and Tribune Company. Reprinted with permission.*

The How and Why of Voting

In the United States, any citizen aged 18 or over is an **eligible voter**. Before a person can vote, he or she must register. People register before voting for the first time and whenever they move. Registration of voters is handled by the county government. Voting is done at a polling place, where voters' names are checked against a registration list. People vote privately in an enclosed voting booth; or, if they are unable to go to a polling place, they may vote by absentee ballot.

A few states conduct some elections by mail. Proposals also have been made to use the Internet for voting. In fact, some people believe the Internet could be used not only for elections, but to bring more citizen participation to government. Citizens could follow a city council meeting on-line, and then instantly register their opinions about the issues being discussed through e-mail.

The United States is a representative democracy, in which power belongs to the people. Voters elect many of the government officials who are responsible for making, enforcing, and interpreting laws. These government officials obtain their power from the voters. The best way for people in the United States to exercise their power is through voting.

Yet many Americans don't vote. In the 1996 presidential election, **voter turnout** was less than 50 percent. That means less than half of the registered voters cast ballots. The percentage of voters was even smaller when compared to the number of *eligible* voters, which includes people who could register but do not.

It all adds up to this: Millions of Americans who could vote don't bother. Yet how many of the non-voters complain about what our elected leaders do?

The Electoral College

Did you know that American voters don't really elect the president? The president is actually chosen by the Electoral College. Each state gets a number of electoral votes equal to its number of U.S. senators and representatives. (Virginia currently has 13; California, with 54, has the most.) In any state, the candidate getting the largest number of popular votes (cast by citizens) usually gets all of the state's electoral votes. A candidate needs a majority of electoral votes (270 out of a total of 538) to win the presidency.

Today, a candidate could be elected by winning the 12 biggest states, which have 281 electoral votes between them. It wouldn't matter what happened in the other 38 states. In fact, the electoral college system means it's possible for a candidate to become president without winning the popular vote. Couldn't happen? It already has: in 1884, 1876, and 1824.

The Founding Fathers created the Electoral College in part because they mistrusted the voters to pick good presidents. In the early years, members of the Electoral College could vote for any candidate they chose. Today, state laws often require a state's electors to vote for the candidate with the largest popular vote.

What Do You Think?

Directions: Answer the questions on the lines provided. Be prepared to discuss your answers in class.

1. Read the following passage.

   According to the Virginia Constitution, the General Assembly has the right to elect state judges. They are never required to be approved by the voters themselves. In many other states, judges must run for reelection every few years. If the voters don't want them to serve, they lose their jobs.

   Which is better? Should judges face the voters directly every few years, or should they be elected by the General Assembly? Give reasons for your answer.

   _____

   _____

   _____

   _____

   _____

   _____

2. Name some ways in which the media can influence elections, not including the fact that they carry advertising for candidates.

   _____

   _____

   _____

   _____

   _____

   _____

Test Your Knowledge

Directions: Match the definitions below to the correct terms.

_____ 1. Division of governmental power into three branches

_____ 2. Ability of each branch to hold back the power of another

_____ 3. Supreme and lower courts

_____ 4. U.S. House of Representatives and Senate, Virginia General Assembly

_____ 5. President or governor

    A. Legislative branch
    B. Checks and balances
    C. Separation of powers
    D. Executive branch
    E. Judicial branch

Directions: Fill in the blanks in each statement below.

6. In the Virginia General Assembly, there are 40 _____ and 100

    _____.

7. In Virginia, the governor _____ the top officials of some state offices, who serve in his cabinet.

8. The _____ of Virginia, the highest court in the commonwealth, has seven members.

Directions: Write a short definition of each term on the lines below.

9. Political party:

    _____

    _____

    _____

    _____

10. Platform:

_____

_____

_____

_____

_____

_____

11. Primary election:

_____

_____

_____

_____

_____

_____

12. Voter turnout:

_____

_____

_____

_____

_____

Unit 4 Review Test

1. Roots of the Declaration of Independence can be found in all the following historic documents except the
   A. Magna Carta.
   B. Treaty of Paris.
   C. Mayflower Compact.
   D. English Bill of Rights.

2. Which of the following statements below is not part of the Declaration of Independence?
   A. All people are created equal.
   B. The U.S. government will have three branches.
   C. People form governments to protect their rights.
   D. People have the right to life, liberty, and the pursuit of happiness.

3. According to the Declaration of Independence, what can people do if their form of government no longer works?
   A. nothing
   B. change the government
   C. vote for a new representative
   D. separate from Great Britain

4. Which American document was written to establish justice, provide for the common defense, and secure the blessings of liberty for Americans?
   A. Magna Carta
   B. Articles of Confederation
   C. Declaration of Independence
   D. Constitution of the United States

5. The first 10 amendments to the Constitution are called the
   A. Articles of Confederation.
   B. Emancipation Proclamation.
   C. Bill of Rights.
   D. Declaration of Independence.

6. Which right listed below is part of the Second Amendment?
   A. right to keep guns
   B. right to free speech
   C. right to a fair trial in court
   D. right to be free from searches

March 9th: Congress passes a law making it illegal to keep certain types of guns from being sold in the United States.

March 16th: The president, opposed to the gun bill, officially vetoes it.

March 23rd: The gun bill passed by Congress on March 9th becomes law.

7. What most likely happened between March 16th and March 23rd?
   A. The Supreme Court approved the gun bill.
   B. Congress voted to override the president's veto.
   C. The president changed his mind and signed the bill.
   D. The governors of the states demanded that the bill become law.

8. This interaction between Congress and the president is called
   A. rule of law.
   B. majority rule.
   C. judicial review.
   D. checks and balances.

9. Who passes state laws in Virginia?
   A. supervisors
   B. the cabinet
   C. the governor
   D. the General Assembly

10. Who can throw out a Virginia law by declaring it to be unconstitutional?
    A. the General Assembly
    B. the Supreme Court of Virginia
    C. any citizen of Virginia
    D. the president of the United States

Kennedy and Nixon

Directions: Look at the chart and graph, then use them to answer Number 11.

11. Kennedy received 49.7 percent of the popular vote and 56.4 percent of the electoral college vote. What is the best explanation for how this could have happened?

    A. Voter turnout was low.

    B. Kennedy won large states by small margins.

    C. Byrd took away Nixon's electoral college votes.

    D. Byrd took away popular votes from Kennedy.

12. Although he lost to Kennedy in 1960, Nixon was elected president in 1968. In 1974, he was accused of committing crimes while in office and resigned. How could he have been removed from office if he had not resigned?

    A. He could not have been removed from office before his term ended.

    B. The Supreme Court could have declared that he must leave office.

    C. Congress could have removed him through the impeachment process.

    D. The governors of the states could have asked Congress to remove him.

Popular Vote for President, 1960

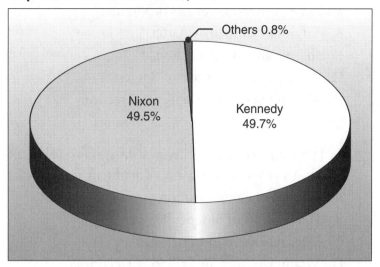

Electoral Vote for President, 1960

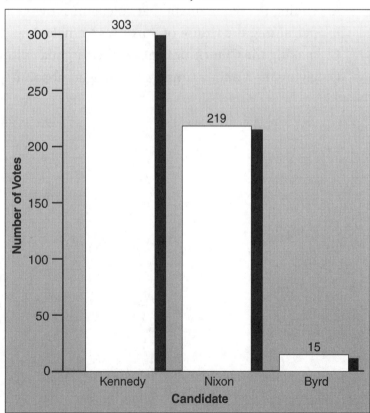

Above: *The 1960 presidential election was one of the closest ever. Democrat John F. Kennedy defeated Republican Richard Nixon. Senator Harry F. Byrd of Virginia received votes in the electoral college, although he was not officially a candidate for president.*

13. Which of the following took power away from the managers of the Virginia Company and gave it to the colonists of Virginia?

    A. Virginia Company Charter

    B. first Virginia Constitution, 1776

    C. creation of the House of Burgesses

    D. Virginia Statute for Religious Freedom

14. In 1776, George Mason wrote a document whose ideas found their way into the Bill of Rights 15 years later. Mason's document was called the

    A   Articles of Confederation.

    B. Declaration of Independence.

    C. Virginia Declaration of Rights.

    D. Virginia Statute for Religious Freedom.

15. Which of the following most expands "consent of the governed"?

    A. ending the requirement that voters must own land

    B. permitting the House of Burgesses to make laws for Virginia

    C. making the Church of England the Virginia colony's official church

    D. giving the Virginia Company managers absolute power over colonists

APPENDIX

- Test-Taking Tips
- Virginia Standards of Learning for Grades 5–7, History and Social Science

Test-Taking Tips

There's no substitute for knowledge when you take a test. You'll get the best results if you know the material that's being tested. But even knowing the material may not be enough if you don't feel comfortable taking tests. That's where a little test preparation can help you.

Most people don't know *everything* there is to know about a subject. They usually know *something* about it, though. Studying will help you gain new knowledge. Test preparation will help you make better use of the knowledge you gain. Both are important.

Inside the Test

The Virginia History and Social Science test is made up of 60 multiple-choice items. There are no other kinds of questions on the test. No matching, no essays, nothing but multiple choice.

Multiple-choice **items** (problems or questions) are made up of a **stem** and four **responses** (sometimes called **answer choices** or **foils**). You will see two kinds of stems on the test.

1. Who was the thirteenth president of the United States?
   A. George Bush
   B. Abraham Lincoln
   C. Millard Fillmore
   D. Thomas Jefferson

or:

1. The thirteenth president of the United States was —
   A. George Bush.
   B. Abraham Lincoln.
   C. Millard Fillmore.
   D. Thomas Jefferson.

Each item has one correct answer choice. At times, you might believe two choices are correct, but only one of them will be correct.

(The correct answer to item 1 is C, Millard Fillmore, who was president from 1850 to 1853.)

Increasing Your Chances for Success

Here's how to attack multiple-choice items.

Imagine that you have just read a test item with four answer choices that looks something like this:

2. Kjfzklf jklas jrljawk l34jlk 3ujoi?
   A. jkfjkjeiosr   C. omelrj
   B. jies   D. 324u4i

Unless you speak the language of whatever planet this item came from, you don't have a chance. You don't know what the question is, let alone what the answer choices mean. There's only one thing to do. You've got to guess.

If you guess, what are your odds of choosing the correct answer? They're not too great—only one in four, or 25 percent. That's not good enough to pass the test, if all the items are as impossible as this one.

Tip 1: ZAP® It!

Chances are that even on the hardest questions, you won't be stumped as badly as you were by Number 2. You'll usually know a little something about either the question or the answer choices. So, instead of taking blind guesses on tough questions, learn to "Zero In And Pick"—ZAP—before you guess.

Look at the next example:

3. In 1792, which was the largest city in the United States?
   A. Cincinnati, Ohio
   B. New York, New York
   C. Boston, Massachusetts
   D. Philadelphia, Pennsylvania

Another tough one. Look carefully at the answer choices.

Philadelphia, Boston, and New York were all cities in colonial days. They're all on the East Coast, in the original 13 states. What about Cincinnati? Ohio was new territory in 1792. There couldn't have been very many people there yet. ZAP choice A.

Okay, so you've ZAPPED one answer choice. Your odds have just gotten better. Instead of a one in four chance of being right on a blind guess, your chances are now one in three. Improving your odds on a single item may not seem like a big deal, but improving your odds on the entire test may make the difference between passing and failing.

Now that you know ZAPPING improves your chances, let's zero in on using it for multiple-choice tests.

Getting the Best of a Multiple-Choice Test

Tip 2: Read every item carefully.

You can't get an item right if you don't know what it's asking. Read carefully to make sure you understand. You may need to read it more than once, but don't spend all morning on the same stem. If you can't understand it after two or three readings, you're probably better off going on to the rest of the test. The lightbulb in your head may start to glow after you turn the page. You can always go back to answer it.

Tip 3: Read all the choices carefully.

It's a mistake to pick the first choice because it sounds okay. One of the other choices may be better.

Tip 4: If there is a map, graph, chart, list, picture, or written passage that goes with the item, look at it carefully, too.

Such material contains information you will need to answer the item.

Often, the test will give you a map, graph, chart, list, picture, or written passage followed by two or more multiple-choice items related to the same material. Don't be surprised when you see them. These items aren't any easier or any harder than any other items on the test.

Tip 5: Once you've ZAPPED a choice, don't consider it again.

When you ZAP a choice, cross off its letter in your test booklet (*not* on your score sheet, where you can't make any extra marks). If you can't decide between the ones remaining and have to come back to it, you won't waste time looking at the choices again.

Tip 6: If you can't ZAP, don't guess right away.

Mark an X next to the item and go on. Sometimes an item will seem clearer or easier to answer if you come back to it later. It's also possible that another item on the test will give you a clue to the correct answer.

Tip 7: Don't leave any blanks on your score sheet.

There's no penalty for getting an item wrong. If you're completely stumped, take a blind guess. You might get it right.

Attacking the Whole Test

Here are some tips for making the most of your time.

Tip 8: Do the easy items first.

If an item seems really hard, mark an X next to it and go on. Plan to come back to it later. This way, you give yourself all the time you need for the hard items by doing the easier ones first.

Tip 9: Check your work.

When you finish the test, you'll feel as if your brain needs a rest, but don't shut it down too soon. Go back to the beginning of the test and make sure you've answered all the questions and that you've filled in your score sheet correctly.

The Last Word

Tip 10: Relax.

The test is important, and it's normal to be a little nervous about it. (If you've studied the material in this book, you shouldn't feel quite so nervous.) If you feel yourself getting stressed out during the test, don't panic. Take a deep breath and blow it out. Stretch. Look out the window for a moment (not too long, though). Then look for an easy question and you'll be back on track.

Virginia Standards of Learning for Grades 5–7, History and Social Science

Buckle Down on Viginia History and Social Science, Book 8, covers the Grades 5–7 skills tested by the Virginia Standards of Learning Assessment Program. Below, workbook lessons are matched to specific Standards of Learning.

Reporting Category: History: First Contact to 1877

Grade Five SOLs in this Reporting Category (reviewed in Lessons 1–8):

5.2 The student will trace the routes and evaluate early explorations of the Americas, in terms of

  (a) the motivations, obstacles, and accomplishments of sponsors and leaders of key expeditions from Spain, France, Portugal, and England;

  (b) the political, economic, and social impact on the American Indians; and

  (c) the economic, ideological, religious, and nationalist forces that led to competition among European powers for control of North America.

5.3 The student will describe colonial America, with emphasis on

  (a) the factors that led to the founding of the colonies, including escape from religious persecution, economic opportunity, release from prison, and military adventure;

  (c) life in the colonies in the 18th century from the perspective of large landowners, farmers, artisans, women, and slaves;

  (d) the principal economic and political connections between the colonies and England;

  (e) sources of dissatisfaction that led to the American Revolution;

  (f) key individuals and events in the American Revolution including King George, Lord North, Lord Cornwallis, John Adams, Samuel Adams, Paul Revere, Benjamin Franklin, George Washington, Thomas Jefferson, Patrick Henry, and Thomas Paine; and

  (g) major military campaigns of the Revolutionary War and reasons why the colonies were able to defeat the British.

5.5 The student will describe challenges faced by the new United States government, with emphasis on

  (b) major issues facing Congress and the first four presidents.

5.6 The student will describe growth and change in America from 1801 to 1861, with emphasis on

  (a) territorial exploration, expansion, and settlement, including the Louisiana Purchase, the Lewis and Clark expedition, the acquisition of Florida, Texas, Oregon, and California; and

  (c) the principal relationships between the United States and its neighbors (current Mexico and Canada) and European powers (including the Monroe Doctrine), and describe how those relationships influenced westward expansion.

5.7 The student will identify causes, key events, and effects of the Civil War and Reconstruction, with emphasis on

  (b) events leading to secession and war;

  (c) leaders on both sides of the war, including Abraham Lincoln, Ulysses S. Grant, Jefferson Davis, Robert E. Lee, Frederick Douglass, and William Lloyd Garrison;

  (d) critical developments in the war, including major battles, the Emancipation Proclamation, and Lee's surrender at Appomatox;

  (e) life on the battlefield and on the homefront; and

  (g) the impact of Reconstruction policies on the South.

5.8   The student will interpret patriotic slogans and excerpts from notable speeches and documents in United States history up to 1877, including "Give me liberty or give me death," "Remember the Alamo," "E Pluribus Unum," the Gettysburg Address, the Preamble to the Constitution, and the Declaration of Independence.

5.9   The student will develop skills for historical analysis, including the ability to

(a) identify, analyze, and interpret primary sources (artifacts, diaries, letters, photographs, art, documents, and newspapers) and contemporary media (television, movies, and computer information systems) to better understand events and life in United States history to 1877; and

(b) construct various timelines of American history from pre-Columbian times to 1877, highlighting landmark dates, technological changes, major political and military events, and major historical figures.

5.10 The student will develop skills in discussion, debate, and persuasive writing by analyzing historical situations and events, including

(a) different historical perspectives, such as American Indians and settlers, slaves and slaveholders, Patriots and Tories, Federalists and Anti-Federalists, Rebels and Yankees, Republicans and Democrats, farmers and city folks, etc.

Reporting Category: History: 1877 to the Present

Grade Six SOLs in this Reporting Category (Lessons 9–12):

6.1   The student will explain how, following the Civil War, massive immigration, combined with the rise of big business, heavy industry, and mechanized farming transformed American life, with emphasis on

(a) Western settlement and changing federal policy toward the Indians;

(b) why various immigrant groups came to America, some of the obstacles they faced, and the important contributions they made; and

(c) the growth of American cities, including the impact of racial and ethnic conflict and the role of political machines.

6.2   The student will analyze and explain Americans' responses to industrialization and urbanization, with emphasis on

(a) muckraking literature and the rise of the Progressive Movement;

(b) women's suffrage and temperance movements, and their impact on society;

(c) child labor, working conditions, and the rise of organized labor;

(d) political changes at the local, state, and national levels; and

(e) improvements in standards of living, life expectancy, and living conditions.

6.3   The student will describe and analyze the changing role of the United States in world affairs between 1898 and 1930, with emphasis on

(a) the Spanish-American War;

(b) the Panama Canal;

(c) Theodore Roosevelt's "Big-Stick Diplomacy;"

(d) United States's role in World War I; and

(e) the League of Nations.

6.4   The student will describe the ideas and events of the 1920s and 1930s, with emphasis on

(a) music, dance, and entertainment;

(b) the Harlem Renaissance;

(d) prohibition, speakeasies, and bootlegging;

(e) the impact of women's suffrage;

(f) racial tensions and labor strife; and

(g) urban and rural electrification.

6.5 The student will explain the Great Depression and its effects, with emphasis on

  (d) personalities and leaders of the period, including Will Rogers, Eleanor and Franklin Roosevelt, and Charles Lindbergh.

6.6 The student will analyze and explain the major causes, events, personalities, and effects of World War II, with emphasis on

  (a) the rise of Fascism, Nazism, and Communism in the 1930s and 1940s and the response of Europe and the United States;
  (b) aggression in Europe and the Pacific;
  (c) failure of the policy of appeasement;
  (d) the Holocaust; and
  (e) major battles of World War II and the reasons for Allied victory.

6.7 The student will describe the economic, social, and political transformation of the United States since World War II, with emphasis on

  (a) segregation, desegregation, and the Civil Rights Movement;
  (b) the changing role of women in America;
  (f) effects of increased immigration;
  (h) effects of organized religious activism; and
  (i) political leaders of the period, trends in national elections, and differences between the two major political parties.

6.8 The student will describe United States foreign policy since World War II, with emphasis on

  (a) the Cold War and the policy of communist containment;
  (b) confrontations with the Soviet Union in Berlin and Cuba;
  (c) nuclear weapons and the arms race;
  (d) McCarthyism and the fear of communist influence within the United States;
  (e) NATO and other alliances, and our role in the United Nations;
  (f) military conflicts in Korea, Vietnam, and the Middle East; and
  (g) the collapse of communism in Europe and the rise of new challenges.

6.9 The student will interpret patriotic slogans and excerpts from notable speeches in United States history since 1877, including "Ask not what your country can do for you...," "...December 7, 1941, a date which will live in infamy," "I have a dream...," and "Mr. Gorbachev, tear down this wall!"

6.10 The student will develop skills for historical analysis, including the ability to

  (a) identify, analyze, and interpret primary sources (artifacts, diaries, letters, photographs, art, documents, and newspapers) and contemporary media (computer information systems) and to make generalizations about events and life in United States history since 1877;
  (b) recognize and explain how different points of view have been influenced by nationalism, race, religion, and ethnicity;
  (c) distinguish fact from fiction by examining documentary sources; and
  (d) construct various timelines of United States history since 1877, including landmark dates, technological and economic changes, social movements, military conflicts, and presidential elections.

Reporting Category: Geography

Grade Five SOLs in this Reporting Category (Lessons 1–8):

5.1 The student will describe life in America before the 17th century by

  (a) identifying and describing the first Americans, their arrival from Asia, where they settled, and how they lived, including Inuits (Eskimos), Anasazi (cliff dwellers), Northwest Indians (Kwakiutl), Plains Indians, Mound Builders, Indians of the Eastern forest (Iroquois, etc.), Incas, and Mayans; and
  (b) explaining how geography and climate influenced the way various Indian tribes lived.

5.3   The student will describe colonial America, with emphasis on

    (b) geographical, political, economic, and social contrasts in the three regions of New England, the mid-Atlantic, and the South.

5.6   The student will describe growth and change in America from 1801 to 1861, with emphasis on

    (b) how the effects of geography, climate, canals and river systems, economic incentives, and frontier spirit influenced the distribution and movement of people, goods, and services.

5.9   The student will develop skills for historical analysis, including the ability to

    (c) locate on a United States map major physical features, bodies of water, exploration and trade routes, the states that entered the Union up to 1877, and identify the states that formed the Confederacy during the Civil War.

Grade Six SOLs in this Reporting Category (Lesson 12):

6.6   The student will analyze and explain the major causes, events, personalities, and effects of World War II, with emphasis on

    (f) major changes in Eastern Europe, China, Southeast Asia, and Africa following the war.

6.10 The student will develop skills for historical analysis, including the ability to

    (a) locate on a United States map all 50 states, the original 13 states, the states that formed the Confederacy, and the states that entered the Union after 1877.

Reporting Category: Economics

Grade Five SOLs in this Reporting Category (Lessons 1, 5–8):

5.1   The student will describe life in America before the 17th century by

    (c) evaluating the impact of native economies on their religions, arts, shelters, and cultures.

5.6   The student will describe growth and change in America from 1801 to 1861, with emphasis on

    (d) the impact of inventions, including the cotton gin, McCormick reaper, steamboat, and steam locomotive on life in America; and

    (e) the development of money, savings, and credit.

5.7   The student will identify causes, key events, and effects of the Civil War and Reconstruction, with emphasis on

    (a) economic and philosophical differences between the North and South, as exemplified by men such as Daniel Webster and John C. Calhoun.

5.10 The student will develop skills in discussion, debate, and persuasive writing by analyzing historical situations and events, including

    (b) different evaluations of the causes, costs, and benefits of major events in American history up to 1877 such as the American Revolution, the Constitutional Convention, the Civil War, Reconstruction, etc.

Grade Six SOLs in this Reporting Category (Lessons 11–15):

6.3   The student will describe and analyze the changing role of the United States in world affairs between 1898 and 1930, with emphasis on

    (f) tariff barriers to world trade.

6.4 The student will describe the ideas and events of the 1920s and 1930s, with emphasis on

(c) the impact of the automobile.

6.5 The student will explain the Great Depression and its effects, with emphasis on

(a) weaknesses in the economy, the collapse of financial markets in the late 1920s, and other events that triggered the Great Crash;

(b) the extent and depth of business failures, unemployment, and poverty; and

(c) the New Deal and its impact on the Depression and the future role of government in the economy.

6.7 The student will describe the economic, social, and political transformation of the United States since World War II, with emphasis on

(c) the technology revolution and its impact on communication, transportation, and new industries;

(d) the consumer economy and increasing global markets; and

(g) the impact of governmental social and economic programs and the Cold War on the growth of federal income tax revenues and government spending and the role of the Federal Reserve System.

Grade Seven SOLs in this Reporting Category (Lessons 13–15):

7.6 The student will explain the structure and operation of the United States economy as compared with other economies, with emphasis on

(a) the basic concepts of free market, as described by Adam Smith, and of communism, as described by Karl Marx;

(b) the concepts of supply and demand, scarcity, choices, trade-offs, private ownership, incentives, consumer sovereignty, markets, and competition;

(c) private and public financial institutions;

(d) the economic impact of consumption, saving and investment, and borrowing by individuals, firms, and governments; and

(e) the differences between free market, centrally planned, and mixed economies.

7.7 The student will describe the role of government in the United States economy, with emphasis on

(a) provision of public goods and services;

(b) protection of consumer rights, contracts, and property rights;

(c) the impact of government taxation, borrowing, and spending on individuals and on the production and distribution of goods and services; and

(d) the role of the Federal Reserve System and the impact of monetary policy on the money supply and interest rates.

7.8 The student will compare the American political and economic system to systems of other nations, including Japan, China, and leading Western European nations, in terms of

(a) governmental structures and powers;

(b) the degree of governmental control over the economy; and

(c) entrepreneurship, productivity, and standards of living.

7.9 The student will demonstrate an understanding of the rights and responsibilities of citizens in America by

(b) describing and evaluating common forms of credit, savings, investments, purchases, contractual agreements, warranties, and guarantees; and

(c) analyzing career opportunities, in terms of individual abilities, skills, and education and the changing supply and demand for those skills in the economy.

7.10 The student will interpret maps, tables, diagrams, charts, political cartoons, and basic indicators of economic performance (gross domestic product, consumer price index, productivity, index of leading economic indicators, etc.) for understanding of economic and political issues.

Reporting Category: Civics

Grade Five SOLs in this Reporting Category (Lessons 4, 8, 16, 17):

5.4   The student will analyze the United States Constitution and the Bill of Rights, in terms of

(a) the British and American heritage, including the Magna Carta, the English Bill of Rights, the Mayflower Compact, the Virginia Statute of Religious Freedom, and the Articles of Confederation;

(b) the philosophy of government expressed in the Declaration of Independence; and

(c) the powers granted to the Congress, the President, the Supreme Court, and those reserved to the states.

5.5   The student will describe challenges faced by the new United States government, with emphasis on

(a) the writing of a new Constitution in 1787 and the struggles over ratification and the addition of a Bill of Rights; and

(c) conflicts between Thomas Jefferson and Alexander Hamilton that resulted in the emergence of two political parties.

5.7   The student will identify causes, key events, and effects of the Civil War and Reconstruction, with emphasis on

(f) the basic provisions and postwar impact of the 13th, 14th, and 15th Amendments to the United States Constitution.

Grade Six SOLs in this Reporting Category (Lesson 12):

6.7   The student will describe the economic, social, and political transformation of the United States since World War II, with emphasis on

(e) increases in violent crime and illegal drugs.

Grade Seven SOLs in this Reporting Category (Lessons 16–19):

7.1   The student will compare the Charters of the Virginia Company of London, the Virginia Declaration of Rights, the Virginia Statute of Religious Freedom, the Declaration of Independence, the Articles of Confederation, and the Constitutions of the United States and Virginia, as amended, with emphasis on their treatment of

(a) fundamental political principles, including constitutionalism and limited government, rule of law, democracy and republicanism, sovereignty, consent of the governed, separation of powers, checks and balances, and federalism; and

(b) fundamental liberties, rights, and values, including religion, speech, press, assembly and petition, due process, equality under the law, individual worth and dignity, majority rule and minority rights, etc.

7.2   The student will compare the national, state, and local governments, with emphasis on

(a) their structures, functions, and powers;

(b) the election and appointment of officials;

(c) the division and sharing of powers among levels of government;

(d) the separation and sharing of powers within levels of government; and

(e) the process of amending the United States and Virginia Constitutions.

7.3 The student will compare the election process at the local, state, and national levels of government, with emphasis on

(a) nomination and promotion of candidates for elective office;

(b) similarities and differences between the major political parties;

(c) voter turnout;

(d) evaluating accuracy of campaign advertising; and

(e) distinguishing between reporting, analysis, and editorializing in the media, and recognition of bias.

7.4 The student will compare the policy-making process at the local, state, and national levels of government, with emphasis on

(a) the basic law-making process within the respective legislative bodies;

(b) the interaction between the chief executives and the legislative bodies;

(c) the functions of departments, agencies, and regulatory bodies;

(d) the roles of political parties at the state and national levels;

(e) the ways that individuals and cultural, ethnic, and other interest groups can influence government policymakers; and

(f) the impact of the media on public opinion and policymakers.

7.5 The student will distinguish between the judicial systems established by the Virginia and United States Constitutions, with emphasis on

(a) the organization and jurisdiction of Virginia and United States courts;

(b) the exercise of the power of judicial review;

(c) the process of bringing and resolving criminal and civil cases in Virginia's judicial system; and

(d) the function and process of the juvenile justice system in Virginia.

7.9 The student will demonstrate an understanding of the rights and responsibilities of citizens in America by

(a) describing ways individuals participate in the political process, such as registering and voting, communicating with government officials, participating in political campaigns, serving on juries and in voluntary appointed positions.